# PREFACE

If you want to analyze people, the Bible is a good place to begin. It tells it like it is. It doesn't pull any punches—the couples in this book will swear to that!

Some of these couples you know well but others may surprise you. It is just as easy to draw bad conclusions as it is tough to keep from defaming or eulogizing—without justification.

This study has attempted to do neither. It has attempted to tell it like it is, with perhaps an edge going toward giving the benefit of a doubt in favor of a person.

One couple will be presented in each chapter. Certain liberties have been taken, but with considerable restraint. Imagination has played a major role, but in each instance there was something significant which suggested the direction imagination should take. With each couple, one major theme was developed. Because each episode was deliberately designed as an in-depth human and theological study rather than a bio-

graphical sketch, the reader will not find the life story of each couple in this book.

My treatment may reinforce your understanding or it may suggest something completely foreign to you. I have not tried to attempt a far-fetched approach for the sake of effect, nor have I exhausted all of the possibilities suggested by the passages dealing with these couples. If you will read these essays with this in mind, you'll find that a viewpoint different than the one you have normally held will be a refreshing rather than a threatening experience.

There is room for disagreement—lots of it—and if you come up with another angle or a different point of view, great! The thirteen chapters lend themselves nicely to a study guide for a quarter-of-a-year study. You may want to take more time and go at a leisurely pace. The essays vary in length and style, and you no doubt will find them triggering new thoughts on a wide range of subjects.

The couples have been chosen in such a way so that they will suggest many types of people and marriages. Although there is some overlapping, the subject matter does take off in many directions. (Ditto today's couples.) In fact, you may see yourselves here and there, and you will most certainly see many of your friends.

Following each chapter is a series of questions. Be selective. Add your own. Subtract. Allow yourselves to get hung up on one or two questions if you wish. Then, following each set of questions there is a *real life* situation. Put

yourself in the role of a friend, a relative, a clergyman, a counselor, or perhaps even a total stranger—and see what advice or encouragement you could give. How would you back up your advice? Couples everywhere are asking these same questions. There are also a few Biblical references. These are suggestive only, not exhaustive. Play detective and find other passages that will shed some light and give hope. There is a growing library of material on the subject, but be selective.

Read, laugh, probe, weep, argue, and pray. . . . You'll find these intriguing couples are so much like each of us. And age doesn't matter much, either. Engaged couples, newlyweds, salty old timers, and in-laws of every description will find food for thought here. Marriage! Oh, what a wonderful invention. Mankind has tried numerous times to improve on it but without success. Read on!

# CONTENTS

# I

# ADAM AND EVE

## Honeymoons Are Not Eternal

*It is not good for man to be alone.*

Genesis 2:18

Imagine! Love at first sight—and not another living soul around to distract them. A honeymoon in the exquisite Garden of Eden with all expenses paid. No worries about the future. No anxious moments over protocol. And listen to this: not an in-law of any kind—anywhere!

If any marriage was destined to last forever, it was this one.

### TOO GOOD TO BE TRUE

But alas! Anything this ideal must have a catch somewhere. Nothing could be this perfect.

God, in the beginning, created the heavens and the earth. Then, when the time was ready, the creator put forth vegetation; separated the day from night; spangled the skies with soft, twinkling lights; brought forth great sea monsters and tiny little insects and cattle and birds

and beasts of the earth. And God saw that it was good. But He was lonely still.

Then the divine Architect introduced to His world a man called Adam:

Then God sat down—
On the side of a hill where He could think;
By a deep wide river He sat down;
With His head in His hands,
God thought and thought,
Til He thought: I'll make me a man!

Up from the bed of the river
God scooped the clay;
And by the bank of the river
He kneeled Him down,
And there the great God almighty
Who lit the sun and fixed it in the sky,
Who flung the stars to the most far corner of the
    night,
Who rounded the earth in the middle of His
    hand;
This great God,
Like a mammy bending over her baby,
Kneeled down in the dust
Toiling over a lump of clay
Til He shaped it in His own image;

Then into it He blew the breath of life,
And man became a living soul.
A-men. A-men.[1]

James Weldon Johnson

---

[1] *"God's Trombones"* (New York: Viking Press, 1969), pp. 19, 20.

12

Is it possible that God could become lonely? The poet thought so. God wanted someone who could talk with Him, and in the cool of the day, walk with Him. God enjoyed these talks and walks. He still does. When man quits walking and talking with God, it gets pretty lonely. For both. Sometimes man, in his loneliness, gets desperate and tries to find someone else to talk to. And when it finally gets to him, he looks for *something* instead of *someone* to talk to . . . a bowling ball, a bank account, or maybe even a bottle.

Man can get awfully lonesome at times. This is because he is made in the likeness and image of God who, too, can become lonely.

God, in His great, magnanimous spirit, unselfishly caused Adam to sleep unusually heavy one night. When he awoke, Adam soon discovered that his loneliness was gone. He was no longer alone. The Lord God, having borrowed one of Adam's ribs, took of man's own flesh, and with the skill of an eternal Physician, created the zenith of celestial design. Then the Lord God brought this glorious stranger to Adam and said, "Adam, it is not good for you to be alone."

The man, overwhelmed by God's graciousness and Eve's beauty, humbly accepted her as God's perfect gift to him—a helpmeet, a companion, a wife, a lover, a mother. And God looked on that which He had made and saw that it was good.

Then the man said, "This at last is bone of my bone and flesh of my flesh; She shall be called Woman, because she was taken out of Man."

Therefore a man leaves his father and mother and cleaves to his wife, and they become one flesh. The man called his wife Eve because she was the mother of all living.

## PRIVILEGES AND RESPONSIBILITIES

Adam and Eve, in exchange for their honeymoon in the land of Eden, were given certain privileges and responsibilities. As long as they fulfilled their obligations, their honeymoon continued.

Adam's duties were clear enough: "Be fruitful and multiply, and fill the earth, and subdue it; and have dominion over the fish of the sea and over the birds of the air and over every living thing that moves upon the earth." The Lord God took the man and put him in the garden to till it and keep it.

And the Lord God commanded the man, saying: "You may eat of every tree of the garden; but of the tree of knowledge of good and evil you shall not eat, for in the day that you eat of it you shall die."

Adam had one more responsibility. He was also supposed to take care of his wife. She was a *helpmeet:* not an inferior servant but an indispensable, inseparable part of his life. She was given attributes Adam never had. She picked up where he left off. She was given a body and a mind and a set of emotions unequaled by any man. And he was given a body and a mind and a set of emotions unequaled by any woman. This

14

is not gibberish, nor is it doubletalk. Adam and Eve delighted each other. They talked together. They walked together. They worked together. They talked to God together. They ate together. They slept together. God never intended man and woman to compete against each other. God molded the two bodies into one flesh, for time and for eternity.

## WHEN A DRIFT BECOMES A RIFT

One day—how long it took only God knows—Adam and Eve drifted apart. Why we do not know, but it does happen to most couples sooner or later. Honeymoons don't last forever. It is natural—at least normal—to have moments in a marriage when partners drift apart. What is dangerous is not the drift, but the frequency and the duration of the drift. Or that they are not recognized as a normal part of wedded life.

Each couple must somehow recognize that a marriage needs this kind of rhythm, and the partners must be sensitive in knowing when the drift is beneficial and when it is harmful. A husband needs a night out with the boys once in awhile (within reason). A wife needs time with the girls, too. Even so, when a couple begins to want more and more time alone, when the husband begins to create overtime for himself and the wife joins several evening clubs (social, cultural, academic, and even unnecessary church organizations), the natural drift could be widening into a malignant rift.

Perhaps Adam was out tilling the soil and Eve had gone into the center of the garden to gather fruit for dinner. Who knows? In all probability there was a natural drift apart, but it soon widened into an unnatural rift. This was the beginning of the end of their honeymoon.

## HE SHALL RULE OVER YOU

Not all honeymoons end as abruptly as this one did. Eve had wandered near the forbidden tree, listened intently to the malevolent advice, thought it sounded reasonable, helped herself to some of the forbidden fruit, and offered some to her husband. Adam, who knew the ground rules, willingly helped himself. The next thing they knew they were on the outside of the garden looking in. The honeymoon was over.

But God, lonelier than ever at this tragic estrangement, did not turn His back on these two wayward creatures. The first thing He did was to curse the evil serpent, and then He addressed Himself to Adam and Eve. He warned Eve that she would bring forth children in pangs of pain. He told Adam that it would be a constant struggle against nature just to make a living. Then God spoke to both of them (in effect): "You were designed for each other, not to compete but to complement one another. Now that the honeymoon is over, you are going to need each other—more than ever. You will have children which will bring both pain and pleasure. But whatever you do, never allow them to drive a

wedge between you. All the forces of life—including your own family—will try to separate you from each other. Do not allow it to happen. Eve, your husband shall rule over you. If you are wise, you will let him. Adam, do not lord it over your wife but love her as you love yourself. Cleave to each other, put your trust in Me, and nothing shall put you asunder. Marriage is a great mystery, and like love, is designed to last for ever."

Honeymoons do not last forever, but they can be revived, even after long years of marriage, even after all human hope is gone.

*It is not good for man to be alone.*

1. What did God mean when He said, "It is not good for man to be alone"?
2. What can happen to people who live alone? What can marriage do to help bring out the natural aspects of the human personality? What can it do to tone down the eccentricities? Is this a legitimate function of marriage?
3. Why do honeymoons come to an end? What brings newlyweds from the bliss of a honeymoon to the nitty-gritty of marriage?
4. What does the word *cleave* mean?
5. Was Eve created as a slave, a servant, a helpmeet, a spouse, a companion, or a partner? All of these? Some? None? (How do you define *helpmeet?*)
6. Is it natural for a couple to drift apart? How far? How often? How can a couple tell when their marriage is drifting dangerously?
7. How can a marriage be revived when seemingly all hope is gone? Does this happen very often? What can one couple do to help another couple in trouble? How can one couple help another couple get into marital trouble?

READING FURTHER . . .

Genesis 1:1—5:5; Luke 3:38; I Corinthians 15:45; Romans 5; Mark 10:1-12

A CASE STUDY . . .

Bill and Judy were on the third day of their honeymoon which was scheduled for ten days. Bill received a call from his employer *strongly suggesting* that he interrupt his honeymoon to go on an important assignment. This would take two or three weeks, and his wife couldn't go along. His boss promised to make it up to them later. He also let Bill know that it would be to his advantage not to refuse. They have come to you for advice. PLEASE ADVISE.

18

# 2

# ABRAHAM AND SARAH

## Marriages Are Made, Not Born

*I know that you are a woman beautiful to behold.*

Genesis 12:11

Sarah was a beautiful woman—and remained so for many years. Abraham was wealthy—and became even more wealthy. It seemed almost inevitable that these two would end up together.

Yet, money and beauty are often incompatible.

### HOME, SWEET HOME

Abraham and Sarah settled down early in their wedded life in a magnificent city called Ur. Today it is a dusty stop on the famous Baghdad railway. But not so at the time of Abraham.

Twentieth century spades have dug up many ancient cities, but few like Ur—at the time of Abraham and Sarah. It was hardly a primitive

19

city in the days of the patriarchs. It was one of the most important centers of commerce in the crossroads of the world. Ur was surrounded by expansive fields of corn and barley. Groves of date palms and fig trees stretched endlessly into the barren wilderness. Lush green fields of barley and corn were crisscrossed by an ingenious system of canals and ditches.

In the midst of these glorious surroundings arose a majestic temple crowned by a roof of gold which dazzled the eyes as well as the minds of world travelers coming through on the Euphrates River. This incredible ziggurat, the palatial home of the infamous moon-god Nannar, reflected the advanced civilization of Ur below. Ur was blessed with an elaborate method of writing, advanced mathematical formulas, refined specimens of art, a school system, and houses which almost defy description.

Abraham and Sarah may well have lived in a two-story villa with a dozen or more rooms. A visitor would enter through a small door, wash his hands and feet in a basin of water, and then enter the inner court. Around this court were grouped several rooms: the kitchen, a reception hall, living rooms, private rooms, and possibly a domestic chapel.

The walls were deftly plastered and whitewashed. A stone stairway led to the second story where the family and guest rooms were located. Running water was found in the lavatories. Beautiful mosaics adorned the walls. Vases, pot-

tery, and plush rugs made the domestic chores not only pleasurable but inviting.

Abraham conducted his business here. Sarah entertained their many friends, business associates, and relatives in a setting unequaled by our most vivid imagination.

## WHERE HE LEADS ME I WILL FOLLOW

In the midst of this comfortable urban setting, Abraham announced one day that they had to move on. Moving is rarely a pleasant experience (although it can be both an escape and an adventure).

We jest at times (but with a twinge of wishful thinking?) that the wedding ceremony should be amended to include these frivolous words:

> Where he leads me I will follow;
> What she feeds me I will swallow.

This sage bit of advice may not be as irreverent as it sounds. At times it is not easy to follow the leading of a husband (or corporate dictums). Since the mid 1940s the mobility of our culture has increased at an awesome rate. And with it has come a myriad of repercussions, both good and bad.

Exactly how difficult it was for Sarah to pry herself away from the comfort and ease of her lovely home in Ur and to move on to Haran with her husband we do not know.

## TWO TIMES AND OUT

Abraham and Sarah, together with Terah and Lot, left Ur and settled down in Haran, not as majestic as Ur but hardly a primitive village. Then, once again, Abraham informed Sarah that they were leaving. This time their destination was unknown. The Lord God had revealed to Abraham that he was to "go from his country and his kindred and his father's house to the land that I, the Lord God, would show him." More than that, God promised Abraham, already seventy-five years of age, that he would be the father of a great nation. And so Abraham and Sarah left the life of the city and became wandering nomads, living off the frugalities of the wilderness while amassing an even greater fortune.

Success followed Abraham wherever he went. Ironically, his fame and fortune were doubtless softened considerably by living as they did. A tent, no matter how elegant, hardly compares with a two-story villa surrounded by date palms. Gracious living, even though well afforded by affluence, is difficult in the wilderness, especially after having tasted the sweet wine of comfortable cosmopolitan life.

## WHAT LIES AHEAD?

Fortunately for Abraham and Sarah—maybe especially for Sarah—they knew not what lay

before them. Nor do we. It was even more important that Abraham and Sarah had agreed that life together—regardless of the circumstances—was better than being separated. Living together in the wilderness in the will of the Lord God was also infinitely better than living in comfortable Ur without Him.

Sarah made the wonderful discovery that love is sharing your life with your lover. *Where he leads me I will follow* was very real to Sarah. Marriage is beautiful when two wills are merged into one. Marriage is perfect when this will is right in the center of God's will.

## THE OTHER SIDE OF THE COIN

Mature marriages are never the product of one partner simply giving in to the other. Compromises are necessary to be sure, but marriage should not be a perpetual compromise. It would be an injustice to assume that Sarah's magnanimous spirit was the major source of the vitality of their marriage. Knowing some of her frailties assures us that she was quite human—and rather difficult to live with at times.

It is even possible that she was glad to get out of Haran. It is not always pleasant living with relatives, hovering beneath the shadow of a patriarchal father, or even being responsible for a less than grateful nephew. Terah, Abraham's father, and Abraham no doubt had more than one unpleasant moment. It is difficult to imag-

23

ine a perfectly tranquil household dominated by two strong personalities—one, an idolater; the other, a God-fearing son.

## ABRAHAM LOVED SARAH

Abraham, without a doubt, dearly loved his wife. When they left Haran, they were childless. And, by our standards, they were not newly-weds. Abraham had already lived three quarters of a century and Sarah had lived almost that long. However, this being a patriarchal era, it is reasonable to assume that both Abraham and Sarah should be considered much younger physically than their chronological age suggests. This would make Sarah comparable, perhaps, to a woman in her thirties today, an age when physical beauty and womanly charm begin to reach perfection.

Sarah's beauty was more than physical. She had the poise of many sophisticated years of urban living. She had the maturity that comes from living between the awesome tensions of godliness and paganism struggling for supremacy. She knew both worlds, and chose the God of her husband, rejecting the idolatry of her pagan relatives.

It was this woman—unusually beautiful to behold with an inner charm which drew others unto herself—that Abraham loved dearly.

Twice Abraham was desperately afraid of losing her. Both times he tried to save his marriage by insisting that she was his sister, not his

wife. She was, in fact, his half-sister (the daughter of Abraham's father but not his mother). To us this smacks of something highly irregular but at that time it was customary, although it was gradually phased out over the centuries. At any rate, Abraham gambled—twice—in order to save his marriage.

The reasoning behind his deception seems to be this. They had gone to take refuge in Egypt because of the severe famine in Canaan and if the king of Egypt took a liking to Sarah, he could simply eliminate Abraham and add Sarah to his harem. But, if the king thought Sarah was Abraham's sister, he wouldn't have to kill Abraham. He would simply appropriate her. Then, when the timing was right, Abraham would have figured a way to get Sarah back.

This is exactly what happened, except that God bailed them out both times. If we didn't know the character of Abraham, we would say that he was more concerned for his own life than for his marriage. This would not be a fair assessment, however. Abraham was not this kind of a man. He certainly feared losing his own life but he was more afraid of losing her. What agony they must have suffered during those awful moments of separation. This kind of love is easy to return.

Sarah knew that she was loved. She also knew Abraham's heart was breaking when she was led away. She had been a part of the momentous decision they had just made: should they remain where they were and starve or run the risk of

Egypt and live? It was this kind of love that drew Sarah from the luxuries of urban life into the agonies of the wilderness.

A good marriage is not a one-way love affair, nor is it a ritual of acquiescence. Yes, many marriages have been held together by undying one-way torrents of love or meek surrenders. But a marriage like that would have torn Abraham and Sarah apart long before Isaac made his appearance.

No greater thing can a man do for his wife than to love her—and to love her well.

> Where he leads me I will follow;
> What she feeds me I will swallow.

Farfetched? Irreverent? Foolish? Ask Abraham and Sarah.

1. What is the significance of the title of this chapter?
2. How were Abraham and Sarah able to make the difficult adjustments to their personal lives and marriage? Can any couple change their life style if called upon to do so?
3. Abraham seemingly was raised in an idol-worshiping environment and home. How do you account for his godliness?
4. What happens when we want the best of two opposite worlds? What are the blessings to be gained from compromise? Is there a difference between *compromise* and *concession?* What might have happened to Abraham if he had refused to leave Ur or Haran?
5. Was their marriage successful because Sarah yielded to Abraham? When should a wife yield to her husband? (Define *yield* carefully.)
6. What was wrong about Abraham's deception in trying to save Sarah? What was right about it? What else could he have done? Did Abraham fear the loss of his

own life, the loss of his wife, or being abandoned by his God? (What do we know about the Egyptians in this kind of behavior?)

7. Is the rhyme below farfetched? Irreverent? Foolish? Profound?

> Where he leads me I will follow;
> What she feeds me I will swallow.

READING FURTHER . . .

Genesis 11:26—25:11; Hebrews 11:8-19; Psalm 105:9; Isaiah 41:8; Acts 7; Romans 4; James 2:21; Galatians 4:22-31

A CASE STUDY . . .

Judy and Bill have been married now for a couple of years. Bill has been offered a new position in a city hundreds of miles away from home. They do not know anyone there, and Bill has no real assurance that this change will result in a promotion although he feels that the potential is there. Bill feels that he should go; Judy is apprehensive about it and doesn't want to go—deep down she feels that Bill is making a mistake. They have no children but are surrounded with relatives on both sides. They have come to you for advice. Suggestion: CHOOSE A COUPLE TO ACT OUT THE PARTS OF BILL AND JUDY AS YOU DISCUSS THIS.

# 3

# LOT AND HIS WIFE

## Too Much at Home in Sodom

*But Lot's wife behind him looked back, and she became a pillar of salt.*

Genesis 19:26

What an abominable place to live: an awful wasteland; a desert tormented by a strange combination of salt, sand, and sulfur.

But there, in the middle of that nothingness, stood a melancholic monument, an ironic tribute to the abortive fate of a sagging marriage—a motionless pillar of salt.

### AT HOME IN SODOM

When it happened we can only guess, but the marriage of Lot and his wife had begun to sag. Let's go back to the beginning and see if we can reconstruct their situation. Lot, the son of one of Abraham's brothers, tagged along with his uncle from the time they left Ur until they parted company in the wilderness when Lot

28

settled down in the relative comfort of Sodom.

Lot had prospered along with Abraham and, as their herds grew, so did their herdsmen. Since people often get along less splendidly than animals, Lot and Abraham agreed to part company in order to preserve peace. Lot was given first choice and helped himself to the fertile plain not far from the Dead Sea. This left Abraham with the barren wilderness.

Somewhere along the way, Lot married and became the father of two daughters who were probably teen-agers at the time of the fireworks in Sodom. They settled down in a modest little city-state called Sodom, which turned out to be a miserable place to live, much less raise children. But, home is home; and soon both Lot and his wife became attached to their surroundings.

It seems as though Sodom had gone downhill morally, and had reached the next-to-the-bottom plateau on the scale of human dignity. Except for Lot (and his family), who had lived beneath the shadow of a godly guardian for many years, Sodom was for all practical purposes morally bankrupt. The inhabitants had presumably passed through the stage of sexual excess to the inevitable decadence of sexual perversion that follows.

There was only one stage left: bestial satiation. It is from this degradation that Lot and his family (and all Sodom) were spared. It was also in this atmosphere that the Lots lived. They were, unfortunately, at home in Sodom.

# AT HOME AWAY FROM HOME

Home is where a man hangs his hat? Maybe so. Home is where the wife opens the right drawer in order to find a cookie cutter she hasn't used for eleven months? Home is taking off your shoes at night in front of the fireplace and wondering where they are in the morning? Home is where we are comfortable.

Most—maybe we should say many—find it a bit uncomfortable adjusting to a new home. Vacations are great, but a motel room with a thick plush carpet isn't quite the same as home (where the carpeting used to be more-or-less plush).

Lot and his wife and daughters were at home in Sodom. Too much at home! Their daughters were engaged to be married to local home town boys, but these specimens presumably were not much to brag about. Whether Lot and his wife made any effort to find worthy sons for their daughters elsewhere we do not know. Chances are they didn't, judging the circumstances.

Even so, Lot had not lost his sense of decency. He was a gracious host to the strangers who received such an inhospitable welcome to Sodom. He invited them into his home, insisted that they accept his hospitality for the night, and later, when the Sodomites went berserk, he went to the defense of his guests. Seeing the sex-crazed crowd climbing the walls of his house, Lot actually tried to pacify them by offering his daughters. But the mob, young and

old alike, was already too perverted for this overture. Somehow, I wonder if Lot wasn't aware of this but was stalling for time. I hope so, as no man has this right, no matter how grave the situation.

It was then that the guests sprang into action. With the speed of a bolt of lightning they plucked hapless Lot from the clutches of the enraged mob; and with a thrust of his finger, one of the strangers struck the obsessed blind. Even then these depraved monsters wouldn't quit. They groped in their confused blindness until they dropped with exhaustion.

Lot's wife, petrified, watched this episode with horror written all over her face. Her daughters sobbed hysterically, clinging frantically to their mother. Then the guests ordered Lot to round up his future sons-in-law and told him to get them out of there. Lot begged the men to go with him but they shrugged it off. They thought he was jesting.

As the morning began to dawn, the strangers urged Lot to take his wife and two daughters and leave Sodom before it was destroyed. Even then, Lot and his wife stalled. They looked at their home—the treasures of a lifetime nestling on the shelves, hanging on the walls, collecting dust in the attic. Suddenly they didn't want to go. They were too much at home in Sodom! The strangers, refusing to let them turn into ashes, grabbed them by the hand and literally dragged them out of the city.

"How stupid can you get?" we're prone to

judge. But never underestimate the power of a home. It can wrap its tentacles around your heart and squeeze all sound judgment out of it. A home is a wonderful invention, but it can turn on its master.

A question we may never answer is this: Did they dread leaving their home, their lifelong accumulations, and their friends behind—or were they afraid of being at home away from home?? Maybe it was a little of each.

## TRUDGING HAND IN HAND

After the angels had abruptly ripped Lot and his family from their moorings, Lot was still in an argumentative mood. At first he balked when he was told to leave Sodom; then he complained because he had to go so far away. The strangers, not willing to argue any more with him, let him have his way but warned him to hurry. Time was running out. Reluctantly, Lot trudged off hand in hand with his wife, urging his daughters on ahead.

Then the Lord rained fire and brimstone from heaven on the cities of the plain, destroying Sodom and Lot's cozy little villa along with it. The fierce lightning, the stench of sulfur, and the heat were incredible. "Don't look back under any circumstances," they were cautioned.

Mr. and Mrs. Lot plodded on. Mrs. Lot started to lag behind. Lot tugged and pulled, helping her over the dusty trail, almost obliterated by ashes

falling out of the sky. More than once he cautioned her not to look back. Lot kept up a friendly, encouraging patter at first; but gradually it deteriorated into nagging. Then he began to scold her. Finally she couldn't stand it any longer and slipped her hand out of his saying, "You go on ahead with the girls. I'll be right behind you."

Lot, weary of nagging, guilty of scolding, squeezed her hand tenderly and released her reluctantly. Slowly she fell behind. Lot never did look back.

## REMEMBER LOT'S WIFE

Never had Lot's wife seen the desert behave like this before. Ahead of her she could faintly see the figures of three weather beaten people. Not too terribly long ago she had grimaced with pain as she brought two of them into a wicked world—much more wicked than she had dared admit.

Behind her she thought she could hear the awful screams of Sodom. She had a powerful notion to take a look, but just then a low rumbling sound changed her mind. She could feel the earth beneath her tremble. The tremble grew until it crescendoed into a violent eruption. Something awful was happening behind her. She groped blindly in the twilight for her husband's hand. She tried to call her husband's name but no sound came. She did the only thing

she could do—she covered her head with her shawl, closed her eyes, and tried to blot out the wicked scene.

The stench of the sulfuric fumes began to nauseate her. Thoughts of resting for a few moments crossed her mind but she didn't dare. The heat became more oppressive. She could hear screams now when the explosions let up. She knew that she had to move on or she was doomed. Drawing her shawl to the side, she peered into the gloom ahead. Her husband and daughters were in the shadows but she could no longer see them.

Suddenly, a violent explosion knocked her to the ground. All Sodom must have blown up, she thought. As she struggled to her feet, her heart twisted within her frenzied breast. Ahead of her was her family trudging on toward safety. Behind her was her home—her knickknacks—her neighbors—her recipes. She took another glance ahead. When she saw nothing she was overcome —not by the nauseous gas but by a gnawing urge to go back. Slowly the urge overpowered her reasoning. Gathering her garments about her, she pulled the shawl back from her face and slowly turned around, facing the smoldering Sodom she both hated and loved.

## THE TWILIGHT ZONE

All she could see was a cloud of ugly smoke, an eerie spectacle weirdly illuminated by intermittent flashes of lightning and smoldering in

the flames that leaped up from below. As she stood transfixed in this twilight zone, a God directed shift in the wind blew the noxious fumes into the very place where she was standing. Partly hypnotized by the smoldering Sodom, Lot's wife was unable to move. Another blinding flash removed the sight from her eyes. Slowly the deadly fumes closed in on her, snuffing out the last feeble breath from her rigid body.

The savage winds pounded into her, driving the sand and the salt relentlessly against her lifeless form. Gradually the winds died down; and quietly, almost lovingly, nature wrapped the body of the lady from Sodom in a shroud of white. There she stood, a monument to the tragedy of an untimely ending of a marriage. Lot's wife loved well, but she loved the wrong things.

## GROWING ACCUSTOMED TO SODOM

Lot and his wife had many things in common. They both loved their home in Sodom. They were both reluctant to leave. They were both counted as two of the very few righteous in a very wicked city. They had two daughters of marriageable age who were still virtuous in spite of an almost unbelievably horrible environment. Lot and his family, by most normal standards, were decent, God-fearing people.

Yet, something keeps coming to the surface. Their personal lives, their marriage, their role as

parents had taken on an immunity to evil that is frightening. Over the years they had grown accustomed to Sodom. Here they were, living in the midst of a morally bankrupt people. But had they made an impact for good on Sodom? Hardly! Even Abraham, who knew Sodom was evil, had underestimated its wickedness. He asked God to spare the city for the sake of the fifty righteous souls who lived there. Then he revised his calculations: forty, thirty, twenty, ten. . . . He dared to go no further.

We talk glibly that "you can take a boy off the farm but you can't take the farm out of the boy." The same seems to be true of the city. Lot and his wife couldn't get Sodom out of their system.

What does it take to motivate a person—to get him to take action? Lot had two strangers (but not ordinary strangers—even the Sodomites sensed this) mysteriously show up. He was threatened savagely by his neighbors. In desperation he offered his daughters to guarantee the safety of his guests. He watched the ugly mob as they tried to break into his home. He felt strong arms drag him from the mob's clutches. He saw these savages struck with blindness. How dramatic—or even traumatic—could it get?

But even then the angel of the Lord had to drag Lot and his wife out of Sodom. They didn't want to leave; and if they had to go, they didn't want to go very far away. How much does it take to jar a man to his senses?

## DON'T COUNT ON TRAUMA

Ironically, many marriages are predicated on this same folly. "He'll change when we have our first baby. I know he will," reasons a lovesick bride shortly after her marriage to a no-good. "She'll come around when we get out of this dumpy apartment into our own home," muses a frustrated husband. But will they? Chances are pretty slim that even a traumatic experience will make many changes—at least long-term changes. The near death of an infant may sober a young couple into getting squared away with God, but what happens when everything is back to normal? Ask Lot and his wife.

Remember the story told about the nervous bride who was told to concentrate on three things so her wedding would go along beautifully? Just think about the *aisle*, the *altar*, and the *hymn*. She did that and finally it evolved into a little chant: *aisle, altar, hymn; aisle, altar, hymn. . . .* Gradually it seeped down into her subconsciousness: *I'll alter him; I'll alter him. . . .*

Enough has been written about the tragedies in marriages where one partner embarks on a tedious struggle to overhaul the other partner. Or even worse, to remake each other. Imagine the difficulties in trying to overhaul a marriage.

If Lot and his wife were as unmoved by the trauma that moved in on their lives, how much will it take to change us—our attitudes—our

37

habits—our routine—our set ways? The greatest tragedy of Lot and his wife was not the inglorious ending of their wedded life; it was their inability to get out of their rut.

We can hope and pray for something traumatic to happen that will transform our marriage—or change our spouse—or save our children. It could happen, but don't count on it!

*Remember Lot's wife.*

1. How did Abraham contribute to the decline of his nephew Lot? How did he contribute to his well-being? What can we learn from this?
2. Did Abraham offer Lot his choice in such a way that Lot had to choose the best, or was he simply greedy? (Be sure to back up your answer.) What can a couple learn here about nearby relatives and their relationships to them?
3. What was Sodom really like? What would it be like to raise daughters in this kind of city? Should a godly couple think twice before settling in certain communities? What are some of the things a couple should consider when choosing a place to live?
4. It was suggested that when they fled the city, Lot's gentle encouragement gradually turned into nagging. Can a couple tell when this occurs? When should nagging be done? Can anything good come from nagging? (Be sure to agree on a definition for nagging.)
5. What is the significance of Lot's wife being turned into a pillar of salt (figurative or literal)? Is this interpretation plausible?
6. What was meant by the caution not to count on trauma to save or change a marriage?
7. When a marriage needs a tuneup or an overhaul, how do you go about it? When spiritual values diminish, how can they be restored to a rightful place in a marriage?

READING FURTHER . . .

Genesis 11:31; 12:1-5; chaps. 14, 18, 19; Luke 17:26-33; II Peter 2:7; Galatians 5

A CASE STUDY . . .

Bill and Judy did move to the new city, where they soon
settled down. Judy was quite bitter at first and made
things miserable for both of them. Before too long,
however, she adjusted—too well, in fact—for they both
forgot about spiritual matters and found themselves
quite at home with the ungodly crowd of the city. After
awhile, Bill began to realize what was happening to
them; so he probed into his company a little and found
an opportunity to get a transfer. It would not be an
advancement but would change his living situation. Once
again, Judy doesn't want to go. She likes it too well,
even though it is beginning to show negative effects on
their daughters. Bill has asked you to help him convince
her to move. HOW WOULD YOU GO ABOUT IT?
THEIR TWO DAUGHTERS ARE GROWING UP WITH-
OUT ANY CHURCH INFLUENCE OR SPIRITUAL
NURTURE AT HOME. WOULD YOU ADVISE BILL
TO STAY AND CHANGE THINGS?

# 4

# ISAAC AND REBEKAH

## Love at First Sight

*Then Isaac . . . took Rebekah, and she became his wife; and he loved her.*

Genesis 24:67

The only ones who believe in love at first sight are those who have had it happen to them. All the rest are skeptics.

The story of Isaac and Rebekah begins as a beautiful love story—love at first sight. Unfortunately, they didn't live happily ever after. Isaac and Rebekah didn't get to choose each other; Abraham's trusted, faithful servant made all the arrangements. Is this why their marriage went sour? Let's look and see.

### MATRIMONIAL MATRICULATION

In America today, marriage is primarily the result of a courtship, ranging from a dizzying, whirlwind weekend romance to the meticulously drawn out engagement. Statistics may favor

moderately long courtships over the excessively long engagements or the impulsive elopements, but courtship in our culture is difficult to compare with parental matching of the East.

Traditionally there seem to be four major methods of matrimonial matriculation. The first would be the *prearranged marriage* conducted usually by the family. Often involved in these arrangements are economic and political dimensions, but a surprisingly high number of marriages seem to survive in spite of this intrigue.

The next method might be called the courtship marriage, where usually the man courts the woman, they fall in love and get married. How these two people were introduced could have a unique history ranging from "she was the girl who lived next door" to a blind date or a casual chance meeting.

Another grouping could be called the *circumstantial marriage*. Unusual (and routine) situations quite often result in matrimony. Sometimes there is the shotgun wedding, the marriage to save face; marriages at times are the result, not of either prearrangement or courtship, but lie somewhere between the two: an aspiring executive marries the boss's daughter—a violinist marries a pianist—a Rockefeller marries a Carnegie—a Presbyterian marries a Presbyterian.

Finally there is the *computerized marriage*. Not without its faults, the computer has ushered in a brand new era of fascinating (and frustrating) dimensions to love, courtship, and marriage. It is true that a trusted fraternity brother might

be more reliable than an IBM computer, but we won't delve into that.

What it amounts to is this: marriage at best is a blind date. No one can predict the outcome. A man and a woman could court each other for ten years and still make some fantastic discoveries about each other within a year of wedded life. The complex impact of marriage on a person cannot be fully predicted. Even couples who live together out of wedlock—experimentally or otherwise—do not know what marriage actually is all about. In fact, their mutual arrangement can be seemingly quite satisfactory, especially when compared to their friends whose marriages no doubt are less than perfect. Even so, the spiritual and cultural union in marriage is so designed that when these vowless couples do decide to take the marriage vow, their new life together will not be simply more of the old. The mystery of marriage defies an easy understanding. It is a unique phenomenon. The woman you courted is not the same woman you are married to—not exactly. Nor is the man who courted you identical to the person to whom you are now married. Marriage is like a blind date: you go into it with your eyes open but there is a lot you cannot see.

## THE THIRD PARTY

Isaac and Rebekah were both quite willing to rely on the judgment of Abraham's trusted servant. The reason no doubt was partly because it

was the custom, but partly because of the caliber of the servant as well. He knew Isaac well. He knew his interests and his likes, his personality and his quirks. He also knew what was good for Isaac and what would please him. In fact, it is quite possible that this old timer might have done a better job of picking out a bride for Isaac than Isaac could have done for himself. (If we think we are doing so magnificently in our courtship culture, look at the awesome divorce and legal separation statistics. We could possibly use a better method or improve on our existing system, could we not?)

Whom did the servant choose for his master? "Behold, Rebekah . . . came out with her water jar upon her shoulder. The maiden was very fair to look upon, a virgin. . . . The man gazed at her in silence to learn whether the Lord had prospered his journey or not." Rebekah, no matter how you looked at her, was worth looking at. She was beautiful, poised, gracious, friendly, hospitable, thoughtful, and anxious to please.

The perceptive servant watched her carefully, and then bowed his wise old head to ask his God if she was everything she appeared to be. When the servant was convinced that he could do no better for his master, he gave her a gold ring and two bracelets to prove his sincerity. Rebekah was so anxious to tell her family that she ran all the way home.

One of the greatest reassurances we can receive is not only to love and be loved but to know that our family and friends also love the

one we love. This third dimension is unbelievably beneficial (but it can also work the other way, too). If most of your friends and loved ones disliked (or merely tolerated—no real enthusiasm shown) the one you chose to walk through life together with, how did you react? Did your feet grow cold? Or did you dismiss these critics as worthless snobs? How many mismatches have been made out of spite no one knows; nor can statistics be flung at the world about the number of potentially excellent marriages that have been smashed by insensitive cynics.

Somewhere, somehow, a courtship would do well if it could draw on the wisdom and impartiality of a third party, especially if a God-fearing individual such as Abraham's servant was available. This man, a friend to Isaac and Rebekah alike, brought two strangers together who immediately fell deeply in love. Ironically, this same servant could have done Isaac and Rebekah a lot of good if he had been kept on as a trusted and honored party of the third part. Presumably this was not the case.

## WHAT'S BEHIND THE VEIL?

One of the intriguing aspects of a marriage is that both parties know so little about each other. Rebekah was young, eager to find a man who would love her, give her children, and fulfill the desires of her heart. Isaac had waited a long time for a bride. For him, life was about to begin.

As the caravan drew close to its destination, Rebekah's heart began to flutter. Then she saw the figure of a man—tall, sure of himself, handsome—coming in their direction. She leaned over toward the servant and asked, "Who is that man?" The servant replied, "It is my master." Quickly, Rebekah took her veil and properly covered herself. Then the trusted servant stopped the caravan, dismounted, and walked ahead to meet Isaac to tell him the wonderful news. Isaac listened to every word. When he was convinced he was not dreaming, he dismissed his loyal servant, gathered his veiled bride in his arms, carried her across the threshold of his tent, and she became his wife. And the most beautiful part of it all—he loved her.

What did her veil conceal? It could not hide the pounding of her heart, the joys that welled up within her soul, the expectations of her love. It did, however, hide her anxieties. So much had happened, and so much more was to come. Symbolically, her veil hid not so much the Rebekah she was as the Rebekah she would become.

## THE FIRST TWENTY YEARS
## ARE THE HARDEST

There is a lot of talk today about the inevitably brief tenure of the love affair known as marriage. "When the light goes out it's time to strike a new match," we're told. A lot of attention is being devoted to the ancient notion of

marriage as obsolete. We are being told in no uncertain terms that it is not possible and hardly desirable for two people to commit themselves to each other for an indefinite period of time. In fact, it is argued, it can't be done—mentally, physically, or socially.

Actors and actresses no longer are regarded as gods and goddesses in our culture, but they are still regarded as influential and consequently as authoritative. One such individual was interviewed by a leading publication and expressed her sentiments as rather typical of a prevailing mood in our society. She claimed that monogamy no longer makes sense. The natural behavior pattern of man is not monogamous (but it might be to a muskrat). She went on to explain certain statistics of sexual behavior which seemingly reveal that the intensity of the love (sexual) relationship diminishes to zero (or close to it) within two and a half or three years (five years at the most). When a marriage wears out, it's time to get a new one.

Marriages do wear thin. Sometimes they wear out. Physically it is unquestionably true that rather shortly after the honeymoon (three to five years) many marriages do run out of gas. Marriages built primarily on sex (and this is not intended to minimize the role of sex in marriage) get into trouble at a young age. Men and women are not animals; consequently, life must consist of more than merely satisfying biological urges.

Consider Isaac and Rebekah. For twenty years they ate, drank, and made love with aban-

don. He was virile and she was beautiful. He was anxious to have a son and she was eager to be the mother of a special race. There should have been no diminishing of their sexual relationship because of any fear of pregnancy or any physical disability. Finally, after twenty years, she conceived and brought forth twin sons—one destined to greatness, the other to mediocrity.

## MAN SHALL NOT LIVE BY SEX ALONE

Even sex can become boring. Human nature is so arranged that things preferred rather quickly become things common. Take the dilemma of mass communications in reporting a moon landing. Three or four spectacular achievements no longer capture the imagination of the typical man on the street. Baseball is considering revising the rules to rev up the game. Basketball has had the same idea. How many months does it take a young couple (or an older one) before they quit taking every visitor on a tour of their new home—or before we refrain from showing off our new car? How many pictures do we have of our third child?

Marriage is smitten likewise with this malady. Its newness soon wears off, and with it the physical dimensions begin to fade. This is hardly news, but the answer is not to discard a mate like an unloved garment just to start the whole cycle over again. Nor is the answer to stick it out in order to enjoy the unnecessary pain of being a martyr.

This is the route Isaac and Rebekah chose.

47

Their marriage gradually deteriorated until, by the time Jacob and Esau made their appearance, their parents were not only merely tolerating each other, they were actual enemies. Their marriage had passed through the crisis period (the first two to five years) when the momentum of the courtship and honeymoon fades and the pulling power of the marriage itself takes over or else! Physical relationships need not diminish but must take on spiritual overtones. Why? Because man cannot live by sex alone.

## WHAT HAPPENED TO THEIR LOVE?

But love, like matter, is difficult—perhaps even impossible—to destroy. It simply takes on different dimensions. Rebekah became bitter in her barrenness, blaming Isaac, and then God. Isaac found his faith in the God of his father Abraham wavering as the years rolled on with no heir in sight. As they lived with their disappointments, God was crowded out. They began to love themselves more and each other less. Then they had to settle on loving things instead of people, until that gloriously tragic day when Esau and Jacob came to live with them.

When the anxiously awaited twins arrived, they were met head on by parents who had fallen out of love. Esau, destined to forfeit his natural rights as first born, was no match against his scheming mother. Jacob regrettably was spoiled by the same woman. Isaac seemingly was content to live for the savory venison his favor-

ite son Esau provided in season and out of season. Rebekah twisted the world at will so that it would have the right shape for her son Jacob. Isaac just sat and watched it go by. What a setup! A dominating, scheming mother and a retiring father.

What happened? Their love somehow got mangled in the squeeze of life. At first their love was one of passionate devotion with moments of tender compassion. Then came the gradual shift to a life of tender compassion with moments of passion. Gradually both were gone, but the expected spiritual quietude of a mature marriage never became their portion. Isaac and Rebekah never knew this ecstasy.

After twenty long years, Isaac and Rebekah should have had plenty time to prepare for this happy event with a joyous, spiritual anticipation. But they didn't. Instead of drawing them together, the birth of their children only widened the wedge. Isaac poured all of his love into Esau, his first born. Rebekah countered with shrewd manipulations designed to exalt Jacob but at the expense of Esau. It is doubtful that Isaac and Rebekah ever experienced the love of a husband and a wife which can take on an inexpressible new dimension at the birth of their own flesh and blood. There is more than enough love to go around. It doesn't have to be diverted from a husband or a wife. Their love probably wasn't destroyed; it was simply abused and unused. Instead of loving each other more deeply, Isaac and Rebekah spent their love on their

favorite child. This always turns out to be a bad investment, as everyone loses.

## LOVE AT FIRST SIGHT

Was the tragedy of the love of Isaac and Rebekah due to their instant marriage? Long engagements do not guarantee successful marriages any more than quickie ceremonies automatically spell disaster. Isaac and Rebekah had plenty of time to adjust and mature in their love for each other after their marriage. Marriage is an ingenious institution, designed to last not only a lifetime but for eternity. To be successful, however, a couple must work at it together, and sometimes with a trusty, wise, and godly third party. Isaac and Rebekah missed this necessary dimension. Isaac had dismissed his father's highly esteemed servant too soon.

Whenever we think our marriage has *arrived* we discover a new beginning. Marriage grows and takes on new dimensions as it unfolds. When the physical is interrupted or fades, the spiritual increases. When the physical revives it is enhanced, not abandoned, by the spiritual. After awhile it is difficult to know where one ends and the other begins. This is one of the mysteries of love: the more demand there is for it, the more love there is—if you don't let it die.

For Isaac and Rebekah it was love at first sight, but then it faded. Why? We can only speculate, and even then we may be unfair. Perhaps we should remind ourselves of the

earthy wisdom of a wise old parson who talked rather bluntly to a young groom. "Listen," said he, "now that you've caught the fish, don't throw the bait away."

This rather profound analogy is more wise than it is witty. Courtship must continue throughout the marriage; it must not end with the honeymoon. We must go even one step further and not limit this continuing courtship to merely the husband. Both the husband and wife should work at it, just as both of them worked at it prior to the marriage feast. It is not unwise for a bride of yesterday or the wife of a decade to flirt just a little with her husband now and then.

Marriage may be the culmination of a long courtship or a sudden departure from the status quo. In either event, it can result in a long, lovely journey for two. But it will take a lot of hard work—by both parties. Isaac and Rebekah started that journey well, but somehow they took their eyes off each other and missed the road.

*Love at first sight can be a beautiful experience if you don't lose your vision.*

1. Is there such a thing as "love at first sight"? Are there any age restrictions?
2. Marriage, including courtship, has been under severe fire by many critics. What are some of the hangups regarding courtship and marriage in Western civilization (or America)? What are some of the important criteria for a sound Christian approach to courtship and marriage?
3. Does the Bible lay down any rules or suggestions how

51

a man and a woman ought to court each other (assuming that the woman does have a role here)?
4. Elaborate on the four types of courtship-marriage suggested in this chapter: *prearranged* marriage, *courtship* marriage, *circumstantial* marriage; *computerized* marriage. Can you think of any others? Would you add a *providential* marriage?
5. How important is it for a third party to become involved in a courtship and marriage? How can a couple arrange for a third party? Who can best fill this role?
6. Why are so many marriages crumbling today after twenty or twenty-five years of wedlock? Explain: "When the light goes out it's time to strike a new match." Could this hold more than one meaning?
7. React to this sequence in the light of the adage that "man shall not live by sex alone": attraction, affection, passion, climax, ecstasy, serenity (define *serenity* in its deepest sense). Is the last position generally omitted in much secular material dealing with marriage and sex? Can the sequence be changed in order to improve it? Can some of the steps be left out? Which ones? Why?

READING FURTHER . . .

Genesis 17; 21:1-8; 22:1-14; chaps. 24—27; Galatians 3, 4; I Peter 3:1-7

A CASE STUDY . . .

Bill and Judy's oldest daughter has gone away to college and has fallen madly in love with a sophomore. They were both smitten by "love at first sight" and want to get married at the end of the school year. Bill and Judy don't know the boy (they think of him as a *boy*) and are skeptical of any form of instant love. They want to advise them to wait awhile. What arguments should they use? How would Scripture help them? Note: TO MAKE THIS MORE AUTHENTIC, HAVE A COUPLE ACT OUT THE PART OF THE YOUNG COUPLE WHO WANT TO GET MARRIED.

# 5

# JACOB, LEAH, AND RACHEL

## The Benefit of a Doubt

*Jacob worked seven years for Rachel, but they seemed to him like a few years because of the love he had for her.*

Genesis 29:20

When Jacob fell he fell hard. He negotiated with his prospective father-in-law, agreeing to work seven years in exchange for his daughter. The deal was made. After he put in his seven years they began a week of marriage festivities which culminated in the long awaited wedding. When he awoke the following day, he made a horrible discovery: he had married the wrong woman. Incredulous!

### IT COULDN'T HAPPEN—BUT IT DID

You and I say this couldn't possibly happen. But it did! It happens all the time—every day. Men marry the wrong woman and women marry the wrong man. Some do it two or three times—

a few even more. And if the law didn't come to the rescue, some would marry several at a time.

But let's get back to Jacob. How could this happen? A little insight into these ancient weddings might help unravel the tangled mystery. Some say, incidentally, that God was punishing Jacob for what he did to his brother Esau. It might be tempting to think this, but don't! Chalk this one up to Laban, a shrewd operator if there ever was one. God is just, but He is not mean!

Laban, Leah and Rachel's father, was a greedy opportunist. Leah was the eldest daughter—not too much to look at, we're told. Rachel was beautiful; and not only that, she had a captivating charm. Jacob, otherwise quite capable of taking care of himself, somehow allowed himself to get tangled in a deal which cost him seven years. This also gave scheming Laban plenty of time to trap Jacob again.

After putting in seven years of labor for the woman he loved, elaborate plans were unfolded for a gala celebration. Laban could never be satisfied with an ordinary affair. As the days passed by, the exciting festivities—music, dancing, eating, drinking—reached a climax: it came time for the wedding feast, the highlight of the festival.

Here is where Laban rose to the occasion. After seven years Jacob was ready for a celebration. And celebrate he did! Before long he was feeling better than he should. Laban saw to it that his goblet was always full. The sweet wine

never actually turned on him but it did dull his senses enough so that, coupled with the excitement of the hour, Jacob wasn't quite with it.

Later that evening, as it was the custom, Laban escorted the bride, veiled quite appropriately for the occasion, to the nuptial chamber where she was presented to Jacob. Everything was going along beautifully just as' Laban had planned. A small candle flickered in the darkness, giving little illumination but filling the chamber with a romantic fragrance. The mood was perfect. Quietly Laban stole away, leaving the two lovers alone. Leah, trembling beneath her disguise, gently snuffed out the flickering flame, deftly unwound the veil from her face, and led Jacob through the darkness into a night of love. Only when he awoke, hours later, did he realize what had happened.

It couldn't happen but it did!

Jacob did not love Leah. He probably didn't even like her. After this cruel deception, he found it even more difficult just to tolerate her. No doubt he forgot and forgave, to a degree; but Leah never did have the same place in his heart that her sister had, although she gave him his firstborn son and nursed his infant son Benjamin through the hour of his greatest agony.

Treachery as a basis for marriage is risky business. Men and women do trick each other into matrimony with many clever, some diabolical, ruses. Unfortunately, many couples (and scheming parents) do play games with each other—both before and after the ceremony. Marriage is

trouble enough without getting tricked into it.

## THREE IS A CROWD

Jacob lost a battle but the war wasn't over. In return for another seven years of hard labor, Rachel was his. Neither tradition nor Scripture is clear at this point. It is quite probable that Jacob was permitted to marry Rachel right away (after the proper festivities) and then worked off his debt. Knowing Jacob, this is doubtless what happened.

Leah was tolerated, not loved. Even giving her husband a son did not change the situation, although she had desperately hoped it would. It is terribly unpleasant to simply be tolerated, but unfortunately it happens all the time. It is extremely difficult to force a man to love a woman or a woman to love a man. It is equally difficult to force oneself to love another. We admire, respect, enjoy, and even like others with relative ease; but to love someone—deeply and passionately—is beyond mere emotional maneuvering. Man has the capacity to love two or even more wives, but it is doubtful that he could ever love them equally.

Leah, urged by her father and supported by custom, probably hoped and even prayed that Jacob would forgive, forget, and learn to love her. This was expecting a lot, she knew. Even so, her hopes were dashed when she placed tiny Reuben ("see, a son") into Jacob's arms. Jacob smiled but the light in his eyes remained dim.

Her hopes faded even more when her sister, bitter and jealous, pitiful and mean, screamed at her husband, "Give me children, or I shall die." No tent or cottage was large enough for Leah and Jacob and Rachel.

## THE CROWD INCREASED

Jacob, Leah, Rachel, and Reuben were only the beginning. Leah had three more sons: Simeon, Levi, and Judah. Rachel wanted a child so badly that she gave her maid to her husband, and by proxy bore Dan and Naphtali. Leah, not to be outdone, gave her maid to Jacob, and Gad and Asher were added. There were now eight boys, four mothers, one father. Then Leah conceived again and gave birth to Issachar and Zebulun before their first daughter, Dinah, arrived on the scene. Finally Rachel conceived and Joseph was born. The family now numbered eleven sons, one daughter, and five parents. Apparently all this took place in a span of a few years.

During this hectic time, Jacob had to keep peace in the family and match wits with a shrewd father-in-law. Ten times Laban changed his wages. Finally Jacob could stand it no longer. Taking his wives into his confidence, he got them to agree that it was time to get out of there. Rachel and Leah cast their lot with their husband, turning their backs on their father and homeland as they journeyed toward the land Jacob left in a hurry twenty years before.

## LIFE CAN BE AWFULLY COMPLICATED

Why tragedy strikes one family and not another is one of the perplexing mysteries of life.
Jacob seems to have had more than his share.
Jacob, no doubt about it, was at times a rascal.
He bilked his brother for all he was worth. He
fled for his life and matched intrigues with his
father-in-law for twenty years. He lived in fear
of his brother, always wondering if and when
Esau would get his revenge. Leah pulled off one
of the greatest deceptions of all time, and now
Rachel had stolen the idols of her father. Laban,
angry that Jacob had severely outwitted him,
took his kinsmen with him and set out after
his son-in-law. He was peeved because he wanted
to say good-bye to his grandchildren. He was
upset because they left when he was away. He
was furious because Jacob had become rich at
his expense. He was nervous because his household gods were missing.

Jacob was so sure no one had taken them that
he offered to sacrifice the life of the one who
had stolen them. Laban searched in vain but
could r t find them because Rachel sat upon
them, u ng the excuse of her being with child
for not g tting up. It seems as though living by
deception sometimes gets to be contagious.
Laban and Jacob, however, made peace; and
Laban kissed his grandchildren and went back
home. A crisis was averted, but we should add,
not without divine intervention. God comes

through—sometimes in striking ways—when He is given half a chance.

## THE BENEFIT OF A DOUBT

Some believe Rachel took the figurines as extra precaution for the new adventures which lay ahead. She knew the God of Abraham, Isaac, and Jacob; but she didn't want to take any chances. Maybe so.

Others interpret this action as a part of her culture. Since immigrants always take their culture with them to some extent, Rachel was doing the same. The household idols (or figurines) were merely a part of that heritage. This is also a possible explanation.

Another view seems even more intriguing. Because she kept them with her, even sitting on them, implies at least a subtle attitude of willful defilement and scornful rejection of their religious significance. Laban called them "my gods." Jacob responded by calling them "your gods." He further emphasized a contempt for them by calling them "household objects." At any rate, Jacob didn't regard them very highly—at least not religiously.

The following interpretation has captured my own personal fancy. We all tend to believe what we want to believe, more or less. Sometimes we are swift to believe the worst; sometimes we refuse to believe anything until we have adequate evidence. When Jacob suggested to Leah and Rachel that they flee from Laban's estate,

they responded: "Have we still a share in the inheritance of our father's house? Are we not reckoned by him as outsiders? For he has sold us and then used up our purchase price" (Gen. 31:14-15). Both Leah and Rachel found it difficult to trust their own father. Presumably, when Jacob fled from Esau, he did not intend to be gone for twenty years. Consequently he did not take much money with him. This is why he agreed to work for seven years for the woman he loved. Realizing that Laban would not let them leave easily—maybe never—the daughters felt that he had been rightfully rewarded and they now belonged to Jacob. This bridal price was a common practice at that time, at least in some parts of the East; and greedy Laban would certainly be sure to take advantage of it.

Laban had a good thing going. Jacob increased Laban's wealth considerably, for he was most competent. No wonder Laban didn't want to let him go. Therefore, since the idea seems to persist that the actual possession of household goods was in some way connected with the legality of title to a rightful inheritance, Rachel may have abducted the idols to insure the fact that Jacob had paid for her in full. Rachel not only loved Jacob; she belonged to him and with him. Oh, for a love that will not let go!

Rachel, like most of us, was not without her imperfections. It seems to me that we would do well if we were to give her the benefit of a doubt. Love is not suspicious. It cannot afford to be. Rachel, in my judgment, should not go

down in history simply as a thief or an idolater. She was a woman desperately afraid that something tragic might happen to her marriage and in her own way tried to prevent this. Dare we indict a woman for trying to save her marriage? For so loving her husband?

## EQUAL BUT NOT IDENTICAL LOVE

Jacob survived his second crisis. He made peace with Laban, only to run head on into his brother Esau. Fear clutched his soul as he sent a most generous peace offering on ahead, hoping that Esau would swallow his revenge. Evidently Esau had done that long ago as he embraced his brother warmly, letting bygones be bygones. Jacob breathed a sigh of relief and they departed in peace—except that Jacob still didn't quite trust his brother.

Shortly after, Jacob and Rachel were eagerly looking forward to their second child. Rachel had much difficulty in giving birth to her second son. When it was all over, Jacob welcomed a healthy baby Benjamin into his household but he had to bid farewell to the woman he loved so dearly.

Rachel was buried near a small village called Bethlehem, and Jacob set up a pillar there to mark her tomb. As Rachel had adopted the children of her handmaiden and reared them as her own, Leah now welcomed Benjamin as her very own. From that day on, Jacob was plagued with family miseries—one after the other. Out of

these heartbreaking experiences a new Jacob emerged. Rather than curse God he leaned more heavily on Him. And on Leah.

Whatever happened to Leah? Did he ever learn to love her in the way he loved Rachel? Probably not. It does appear probable, however, that she slowly began to fill the vacuum created by Rachel's untimely death. Leah raised Benjamin from the moment he drew his first breath and his mother her last, and Leah gently kissed the tears from the eyes of little Joseph when he cried for his mother. Jacob couldn't forget this, nor did he. Lest we forget, it was Leah who was the mother of Levi and Judah, and it was Leah who was buried in the cave in the field at Machpelah, east of Mamre in the land of Canaan, beside Abraham and Sarah, Isaac and Rebekah, and joined later by Jacob.

## ON LEARNING TO LOVE

Many couples face the same situation Jacob faced. He was married to a woman he did not love. Could he ever learn to love her? Many have married with the best of intentions, only to discover that their dream had turned into a nightmare. Is it possible to love and then fall out of love and then learn to love again? Certainly it is, but often it is not easy. We find it so difficult to forgive and forget—so easy to reminisce on the "good old days"—so hard to swallow our pride—so easy to blame.

No one can speak for Jacob. We do not know

if his love for Rachel ever expanded enough to let Leah in. We do not know if he slammed the door shut on the future and lived in the past. We don't even know if he ever forgave Leah for her deception. This we do know, however: Leah became someone very special to Jacob. Let's give him the benefit of a doubt and believe that he eventually learned to love Leah and loved her dearly—not exactly as he had loved Rachel, but in his own unique and satisfying way. A love, yes, that came from above.

It is so hard for us to remember that the God of love specializes in difficult situations. Jacob's love for Leah was not love at first sight but it was worth waiting for. This seems to be implied in the great honor Jacob bestowed on Leah by numbering her with Sarah and Rebekah. Jacob could have asked to be buried in Bethlehem with Rachel, but he didn't. He wanted to be with Leah. If Jacob, with God's help, could learn to love, we could probably do the same.

*Love is a many-splendored thing—especially when given the benefit of a doubt.*

1. Do people change after marriage? How can a couple guard against this?
2. Is it possible to be forced or tricked into marriage and to fall in love or grow in love later? How probable is this? Is it worth the risk?
3. The Bible sometimes seems to ignore or even encourage multiple marriages, particularly polygamy. Is the true Biblical ideal monogamy? How would you make a case for the Biblical position?
4. When should the love of children supersede love between husband and wife? Why are there so many divorces occurring after the first child arrives? How can children make or break a marriage?

63

5. Can you see many parallels between some of these ancient marriages and those of today? Have we come a long way in marriage relationships? Why or why not? What can we learn from these ancient marriages?
6. What are some of the rewards of giving the benefit of a doubt in marriage? What does it mean in I Corinthians 13 that "love is not suspicious"?
7. Because Leah was buried with Jacob, Isaac and Rebekah, Abraham and Sarah, whereas Rachel was buried elsewhere, does this signify a special place of affection for Leah as suggested in this chapter? Was she buried there because she was his first wife? Do you agree that Leah grew on Jacob and earned a special, though different, favor? Are there different kinds of marital love? If so, what are some of them?

READING FURTHER . . .

Genesis 25:19-34; 29; 37:1-36; 45:1—50:26; I Corinthians 13

A CASE STUDY . . .

Judy was beginning to get suspicious. Bill was spending considerably more time in the office working overtime. On several occasions she had called the office but no one answered. She began to wonder more and more if Bill actually was working overtime. When she confronted him with this, he always seemed to have a valid explanation. One day, one of her friends "slipped" in a conversation and implied that Bill was having an affair. It was still in the gossip or rumor stage. Judy has come to you for assistance. HOW WOULD YOU ADVISE HER TO HANDLE THIS TOUCHY SITUATION? REMEMBER, YOU DON'T KNOW IF BILL IS HAVING AN AFFAIR OR NOT; BUT THE MARRIAGE HAS BEEN DETERIORATING GRADUALLY THESE LAST YEARS.

# 6

# SAMSON AND DELILAH

## Games Couples Play

*Get her for me, because she pleases me.*
Judges 14:3

Samson liked women. Most men do—more or less. With Samson it was more. He saw a woman in Timnath, a small border town, and he liked what he saw. So, he asked his father and mother to get her for him.

This may sound a bit strange, even unmasculine. But that's how they did it in those days. After a fruitless—possibly a relatively weak—protest, they obliged their son so he could marry the heathen woman who pleased him. Matches are made in countless ways. So are mismatches.

Whatever the origin, too often marriage is merely a game couples play.

### ONLY FOOLS MAKE THE
### SAME MISTAKE TWICE

Says who? Is it really true that only fools

make the same mistake twice? It is becoming increasingly fashionable not to marry but to pretend to be married and go through the motions—sort of like playing dolls. It is also fashionable to marry with a built-in escape clause written into the marriage ceremony (or at least implied). In fact, there is a good deal of talk about the folly of first marriages. The implication is to get married the first time for a little experience and then call it quits and get married again because the second marriage has a better survival factor.

For a long time, statistics indicted second marriages because people evidently repeated their mistakes. They still do; but rather than quibble with statistics, elusive as they can be, one fact seems to emerge unscathed: people still play games with each other—married or otherwise. Second marriages can be great improvements; they can also be tragedies. To count on it is a gamble; to marry haphazardly with the rip cord hanging loose in case you bail out is not the way to fly. . . .

Back to Samson. His marriage was about as brief as they come. The story is stranger than fiction. Ancient wedding ceremonies, like those of today, were quite brief; but the reception was more like a seven-day carnival. As in the days of Jacob, they feasted lavishly to the tune of stories, songs, and drink. Samson's bride evidently was a popular girl. Thirty young men, old friends of the bride, were at the wedding. To them, Samson was no bargain. He was an un-

polished foreigner who had hoodwinked the unsuspecting bride.

These boys, peeved because an outsider had moved in on their territory, taunted the sober Samson to stump them with a conundrum. His sullen disposition finally broke into a subtle smile as he gave the boys seven days to decipher his riddle. They were stumped:

> Out of the eater came forth meat,
> and out of the strong came forth sweet.

If they could unravel the mystery, Samson would give each of them a change of clothes. Outwitted and frustrated, the stubborn guests put pressure on Samson's wife to get the answer for them. Either in fear or out of respect (after all, they were her guests), she teased and cooed the answer out of her husband and passed the treacherous news on. Samson came unglued; and in a fit of anger and disgust went out and with his bare hands killed thirty men, gave their clothes to the wedding guests, and went to his parental home to sulk.

Time healed his wounds a little, and so he went to see his wife (with a peace offering). When he arrived, her father wouldn't let him in. He was so sure Samson hated his daughter that he had given her to the best man (this happened to David, too). To make amends, he offered Samson another daughter who, he said, was even more beautiful. This pleased Samson not a bit. "So he went and caught three hundred jackals

(or foxes) and got some torches; he tied the jackals tail to tail and fastened a torch between each pair of tails. He then set the torches alight and turned the jackals loose in the standing corn of the Philistines. He burnt up standing corn and stooks (or shocks) as well, vineyards and olive groves" (Judg. 15:4, 5). The Philistines took revenge by killing Samson's wife and her father. Samson, crazed with rage, declared war on the Philistines and smote great numbers of them.

Her malicious (or was it innocent?) little game must have left an indelible mark on Samson. How could he forget? So what did he do? He turned right around and let another woman run her fingers through his locks until she too unlocked his secret. Only fools make the same mistake twice? Apparently so. But that sort of indicts all of us, more or less, doesn't it? Even though it hurts to admit it, there are times when we must recognize that being a fool is one of the luxuries of being human.

## WEAPONS PEOPLE USE

Men and women have played games and fought each other with every conceivable weapon (and not a few of them are ill conceived). Sex is one of them. Historically (and this certainly includes the Bible), sex knows no limits. Lot's daughters plied the old man with wine so that he would father their children. Shechem, a Hivite prince, dishonored Dinah, the only daughter of Jacob. Tamar played the role of a prostitute and

68

enticed her father-in-law to sleep with her to get her revenge. Samson, sometime after his abortive marriage, stopped in Gaza to spend the night with a prostitute. David killed an innocent man for his wife.

The Bible is riddled with candid episodes, sparing not the single or the married, male or female, saint or sinner. A man dilutes his relationship with a woman by having several wives. A woman retaliates by selling her body or refusing to consummate a marriage. It can be a little game couples play, but it sooner or later degenerates into a game without rules and often without a referee.

We dare not make Samson any worse than he was, nor do we dare excuse his behavior. What Samson does so vividly is to dramatize the rough game couples can play. He hurt and he got hurt. And so did others around him. He messed around and he got messed up. He satisfied his biological urges but nearly lost his soul. He lost his sight but saved his breath. The Bible does not say so, but Delilah was probably no angel to begin with. Samson was playing it pretty loose at this time, and he was rebounding from a broken romance and marriage. This is always a vulnerable moment in a person's life, male or female, young or not so young. Broken hearts hurt, and they often hurt for a long time.

If a woman could be induced to seduce, especially in the game of international security (Samson was an awesome threat to the Philistines), she probably used every imaginable wile her

brain and body could exploit. Fortunately for us, the lessons of the story are less than subtle. We know that their affair moved from a clandestine bedroom scene to a death-and-life struggle of political intrigue. A little of James Bondism in reverse perhaps.

Samson was no doubt a handsome man with the aura of an important foreigner—all so alluring to members of the opposite sex. Besides, Samson was Mr. Big in his country. It was more than flattering for Delilah to have such a boyfriend. Exactly what it took for her to get the truth after playing their little game is anybody's guess (the Bible merely gives the plot). Sex undoubtedly played a major role.

## AN UNKIND WORD ABOUT TEASING

The most noble moral of the story of Samson and his women is not as obvious as the easier lessons generally understood. Samson provides all kinds of opportunities for theorizing. He had a godly heritage which he never did completely abandon. He did, like so many, find that strange women can be very tantalizing, even alluring. Girl watching can be a most pleasant pastime, a rather flattering and harmless game. It can also be a dangerous occupation. It's one thing to look; it's quite another to lust. Samson did both.

And there are other morals—maybe even more important. Samson is a great warning to be aware of our strengths and weaknesses. Samson had trouble with both. So do we. We could go

on, but let's settle for one more thought. Playing games with people is dangerous business. Samson played a game with his bride at their reception. It turned out to be a deadly one. At first it was just a friendly little riddle, a harmless little game. But three days passed and no one had unraveled the mystery. Then the game began to deteriorate until it became a war of nerves. Samson was enjoying himself but his wife was caught between protocol and fidelity. She struggled against one teasing husband and thirty bedeviled men. She finally gave in and won the battle but lost the war. What turned out to be some harmless teasing resulted in the slaughter of thirty men. Revenge set in and then revenge upon revenge ravished the scene.

Later on, after the tumult had died down, the enemy seized a golden opportunity to destroy its bitterest enemy. Again, it started as a game. Samson went along with all the intrigue and teasing and loving and nagging and tears. He thought it great sport until one day Delilah lost her cool and accused him of lying and making a fool out of her. That did it. After having been pestered day after day, Samson forgot that he was only playing a game. The battle was over. Teasing can be treacherous!

Samson lost his power, his girl friend, his freedom, and his eyes in one swish of the razor. He also lost his spiritual strength—what was left of it.

Then revenge struck again. The Philistines won a battle but they were about to lose the

war. It was not enough to imprison Samson and to gouge his eyes out of his head. They sought and found an occasion to make sport out of him by making him the pitiful center of attraction at one of their pagan festivals. Their revenge, irrigated by ample wine, made them merrier than ever. It was in this merriment that Samson quietly breathed a prayer, wrapped his mighty arms around the supporting pillars of the temple, leaned forward with all his might, and brought the house down on all the lords and people who were making sport of a man who had regained his awesome strength.

There were few survivors. There usually aren't many when games people play cease to be games.

People do play games with each other, which may be perfectly all right—if they know when to quit. Samson didn't know when to quit. Neither did his wife nor Delilah nor the Philistines.

## ON KNOWING WHEN TO QUIT

Samson ruled Israel as a judge for twenty years. Four chapters in the Book of Judges couldn't possibly tell the whole story. What we do know is quite pathetic. Some would doubt the authenticity of these stories and ban them as unrealistic. Personally, I think not. Life *is* this way. Not long ago, for example, divorce and remarriage in certain Christian circles was unthinkable (and still is in some). When it did occur, people were excommunicated or it was

hushed up until time healed the wounds. Today, most Christian circles include remnants of tragically broken marriages. Both guilty and not-so-guilty parties (if we dare judge), bewildered offspring, unwed mothers and carefree playboys, problematic in-laws and even now and then a defrocked minister all rub shoulders with husbands and wives who are covering up for bad marriages.

I don't know what Samson said when he talked to God in those final moments in the center of that pagan temple. But this I do know: when Samson finally began to whisper a prayer, God wasn't very far away. He never is. The most amazing game Samson played in his lifetime was not the game he played with the women in his life—or with the Philistines—or with his God. It wasn't games that destroyed Samson. It was his inability to know when to quit.

It might be trite, but let's say it again: *the time to quit is when you're ahead.* We all play games. We need to play games. But we also need to know when to quit!

1. Is it true that only fools make the same mistake twice? Why?
2. Certain authorities are suggesting more and more that novices cannot make good marriages; therefore trial marriages or remarriages ought to be encouraged. What do statistics show concerning second marriages? Does "practice make perfect"? What would happen if remarriages became the rule rather than the exception?
3. Couples do play games with each other. What are some of them? When are these games helpful? harmful? Are Christian couples immune?

4. Someone once said, "I can resist anything but temptation." What does this imply?
5. Samson was acting on the rebound from a broken love affair. What is so dangerous about this? Will time heal most heartaches? How much time is necessary? What else is needed besides time?
6. Samson lost his spiritual strength. What does this mean?
7. In this chapter it was said Samson didn't know when to quit. Can you think of any instances when trouble might have been avoided if a husband or wife had known when to quit?

READING FURTHER . . .

Judges 13—16; I Corinthians 7:1-9

A CASE STUDY . . .

Bill and Judy were now playing games with each other. Judy suspected that something was going on behind her back, but Bill wouldn't give her any satisfaction. She nagged and he teased. Neither knew when to quit. The net result was that their marriage was hurting. It turned out that Bill was not having an affair with another woman but resented his wife's accusations. Judy didn't like playing games and felt that she couldn't trust her husband any more, even though she couldn't prove her suspicions. YOU ARE A FRIEND AND KNOW THE TRUTH. HOW COULD YOU GO ABOUT HELPING BILL AND JUDY PATCH UP THEIR CRUMBLING MARRIAGE?

# 7

# RUTH AND BOAZ

## All in the Family

*Then Orpah kissed her mother-in-law and re-*
*turned to her people, but Ruth clung to her. . . .*
*And so she did exactly as her mother-in-law had*
*told her.*

Ruth 1:14; 3:6

A certain father had two sons whom he supported well, but one day a famine ravished the
land where they lived and they had to depart for
another country. There the sons eventually
found wives and settled down.

Tragedy quickly struck: the father and both
sons died, leaving three grief stricken widows
behind. They were destitute; so Naomi, the
mother of the two sons, decided to return to her
own country. She said good-bye to her sons'
widows and turned toward the west. Orpah,
with tears streaming down her cheeks, reluctantly returned the farewell; but Ruth clung to her
mother-in-law.

# TILL DEATH DO US PART

Normally this phrase is not reserved for wives and their mothers-in-law, but in this case it is. As Ruth, a woman from Moab, and Naomi, a Jewess from Israel, wrapped their arms of love around each other, Ruth sobbed these immortal words: "Do not urge me to go back and desert you. Where you go, I will go, and where you stay, I will stay. Your people shall be my people, and your God my God. Where you die, I will die, and there I will be buried. I swear a solemn oath before the Lord your God: nothing but death shall divide us" (Ruth 1:16, 17).

If all in-law relationships were like this, the world would be a much happier place. Mothers-in-law can be the most beautiful people in the world; they can also be quite the opposite. The fact is, there are just too many miserable mothers-in-law. But Naomi wasn't one of them!

Nor was my mother-in-law. I had a wonderful relationship with my wife's mother—while it lasted. Many, many times I have regretted that my children never had the privilege of knowing her. She was hurtled to an untimely death when a carefree gang of joyriders rammed their alcoholic chariot through a metropolitan red light, senselessly killing two innocent people. The driver was a man pushing thirty. I've often wondered how he felt when he returned those empty bottles.

Ever since that fateful day I have found it difficult to get too uproarious over most moth-

er-in-law jokes. But having known my mother-in-law has helped me know and love Naomi, as I think they had quite a bit in common.

Why would Ruth want to stick with her mother-in-law just to go to a foreign country to live with strangers? If Naomi was such a wonderful person, why didn't Orpah want to go with them? Perhaps it was because she didn't have as close a relationship with Naomi. Certain people find themselves drawn toward each other in a manner difficult to explain; others find themselves indifferent to or at odds with each other for equally mysterious reasons. Orpah could have hit it off with Naomi in quite a different manner than Ruth.

Personally, I think there is a more valid possibility. Ruth was deeply impressed with the God of Naomi; Orpah wanted to go back to her people *and* her gods. Ruth not only loved Naomi, she loved Naomi's God. And she wanted to cling to Naomi, not so much out of desperation or affection, but as a way of leaving her past with its heartaches and idolatry behind. These two women got along so beautifully because they had more in common than their mutual loneliness and bewilderment.

## MORE THAN SYMPATHY

In-laws can make or break marriages—and lives! It happens every day. One day I traveled to a far country and visited my maternal homestead. There I visited with a shirttail relative who

lived in an apartment about an hour's drive from where my mother was born. His daughter-in-law lived with them, along with her sons. Not speaking the language of the Scandinavians very well, it took awhile to piece things together. But I learned that their son had walked out on his wife. They took her side in the issue and welcomed her into their home, where she had lived for several years. This is not rare, I know; but it was a moving experience for me when through sign language, a tiny Swedish-English dictionary, and a couple of misty eyes I got the message. Those in-laws were beautiful people. Oh, what a blessing it is when a couple inherit the kind of in-laws who are worthy of the honor of being called an adopted father and mother (this is just as important the other way around, too!).

Naomi was destitute and lonely, bewildered and bitter. Yes, she was bitter. In fact, she wanted her people in Bethlehem to call her Mara (which means "bitter") rather than Naomi. To lose a husband and two sons is not easy for any wife and mother. In addition she was a stranger in a foreign land, and on top of that she felt that the Lord her God had turned against her. This would be enough to make any mother-in-law bitter and cynical and unreasonable. But not Naomi.

She resolved not to be a burden on her daughters-in-law. They were young, with a future still ahead of them. How could she offer them anything more than sympathy? It is true that those who have mourned can weep with those who

weep, but it is not the same to weep with those who weep as it is to offer something beyond sympathy. In the world today there are unquestionably multitudes of people—beautiful people in many ways—sensitive, mature, considerate and understanding, who can and do give strength and comfort in moments of discouragement, loneliness, grief, bewilderment, and even bitterness. But they can go only so far. Naomi was able to go beyond mere sympathy.

Some time ago my heart was crushed when I received word from across the country that the wife of a very dear friend had suddenly and unexpectedly been promoted to a better but far distant world—terribly prematurely. We sent a word of condolence with a scribbled note saying I would call in a couple of weeks, after the swelling tide of sympathy would have receded a little. I waited and then called rather late one night when I was quite certain that the children had been tucked in. We had a long conversation, during which I could tell that the initial shock was fading and that the second wave of awesome loneliness would soon be settling in. A short while later—three or four weeks, I suppose—I wrote a long epistle, not very profound but rather breezy. It was lonely writing, and my mind drifted off to many of the wonderful times we had had together as couples and as families. Pretty soon a letter came back. . . .

Dear Dan,

What a nice warm feeling I got as I read your

letter. There is a saying that "old friends are the best friends." We should amend that to read "old Christian friends are the best friends." It's good to have you "be there" and thanks so much for the letter. . . .

What can we say when a beautiful wife and mother—and yes, a grandmother and mother-in-law, so young and with so many wonderful Christian virtues yet to be shared with those around her—is so suddenly and unexpectedly summoned home? It is at times like this when we need more than sympathy.

Ruth and Naomi didn't know what the future held, but they knew who held the future. This is when it pays to have a heavenly Father rather than a house full of gods. Naomi, a gracious but heartbroken mother-in-law, was able to offer more than sympathy; and Ruth, a bewildered and lonely daughter-in-law, was able to accept. Beautiful!

## NAOMI THE MATCHMAKER

Usually it's the mother, not the mother-in-law, who arranges matrimonial matters. What role Naomi had taken in getting Ruth and her son together we can only guess. Knowing what we do about her, though, we can assume that she probably made her feel right at home. This could well be the best thing a hopeful mother could do. Nothing succeeds like a good dose of warm hospitality.

When Ruth and Naomi reached Bethlehem,

Ruth wasted no time as she set out to make a living for the two of them. It was customary in those days for those who had enough to share with those who had not enough. (Quite a welfare system!) Ruth went along with others as destitute as she, gleaning in the fields behind the harvesters. The rules were clear: no harvester was allowed to harvest everything. They were also instructed to take wide, sweeping turns at the end of the field to leave even more for the gleaners.

Ruth evidently stood out in the crowd, for Boaz asked his men who she was. Boaz was a gentleman farmer, a man of integrity; and when he found out who she was, he gave orders to his men to treat her extra well. Above all, they were told to keep their distance.

Another interesting custom of the Hebrews—a beautiful one—was a family affair. When a man died, his brother or the nearest kinsman was obligated to marry his widow, both to protect the inheritance and lineage as well as to redeem her from a life of poverty. When Naomi discovered that Boaz was a kinsman of her deceased husband, the wheels in her creative mind began to turn. She conceived a bold plan, sharing it with Ruth, who promised to do whatever she was told.

The plan was an intriguing one. Each year, when Boaz and his men finished harvesting, a celebration followed. There would be great feasting and a time of festivity. Boaz would not go home that night (Naomi knew her people

81

well) but would sleep in the barn along with his men. Ruth, who had already earned the reputation of being a chaste, virtuous woman, was advised by her mother-in-law to survey the situation and find out where Boaz had put his blanket for the night. Then when Boaz fell asleep and all was quiet, she was to go where he was sleeping, gently lift the blanket from off his feet, lie down at his feet, and silently pull the blanket over her—and wait.

This she did. No one noticed her as she lay there listening to the heavy breathing of the well-fed harvesters and their master, Boaz. Then Boaz stirred in his sleep. Ruth held her breath until he spoke softly, asking who was there. Ruth confessed who it was and asked him to cover her with his blanket. Boaz immediately understood and promised her that no harm would befall her. He also promised that he would marry her if the next-of-kin who rightfully belonged to Ruth would not.

Boaz, a gentleman in every respect, gently covered her as she rested at his feet; and she slept until it began to dawn. He then gently awakened her, filled her shawl with grain, and sent her back home. After sunup, Boaz wasted no time. He gathered ten elders of the village and asked them to be his witnesses. Then he waited in the gate of the city until the next-of-kin passed by. Boaz informed him that the daughter-in-law of Elimelech had returned and was ready to be redeemed along with his piece of property. The kinsman agreed to redeem the

property but hedged on redeeming Ruth. Boaz then offered, as next-of-kin, to do so if he would release her. Boaz wanted a guarantee, which caused the other relative to remove his sandal before witnesses as an act of solemnization. Boaz was now free to marry Ruth. This he did without delay, and Ruth one day became the great-grandmother of a shepherd boy who became a king.

## WHAT'S RIGHT WITH A MARRIAGE?

We hear an awful lot about what's wrong with marriage—and there is. Not only marriages but marriage itself is in trouble. Amazingly enough, the ingredients that cause a marriage to fail are the same ones that make a marriage successful. Impossible, you say. Paradoxical, yes; but quite possible (although of course there are exceptions).

This was one of the most unlikely situations imaginable. Ruth was a widow, a foreigner—a Gentile who had married a Jew. Boaz was obligated by law to marry her, and she more or less trapped him because of the conniving of a mother-in-law. Their marriage was hastily executed, although Boaz was actually the number two man (at least by law). In spite of these circumstances, that which could have wrecked their marriage actually saved it. But why? There was something right in this marriage: the people involved.

# BOAZ

Let's start with Boaz. There is something admirable about this man. He was an honorable person. He did not take pity on Ruth who came to glean in his fields—that would be a form of condescension. Neither did he make her prove herself. He did what was right in giving strict instructions to his men not only to take good care of her but to keep their distance. He wanted to protect her. This may smack to some of downgrading womanhood. I don't think so. Both men and women have a way of protecting each other—in their own individual style and depending on the situation. When this dimension of human sexuality fades, man-woman relationships head for trouble. The converse is equally devastating to matrimony—when men and women belittle each other or compete ruthlessly for lack of something better to do. Boaz walked the tightrope, not perhaps with ease but with extreme care: he saw to it that plenty of grain was left behind, but he didn't glean for Ruth.

Boaz probably allowed his men to flirt with her, but he didn't want any monkey business. There is a vast difference between a husband who is concerned about the welfare of his wife and a two-bit loud mouth who flies into a rage when someone winks at his spouse.

Boaz did little favors for her. Maybe he was falling in love by now. If so, what's so bad about that? There is an awesome difference between thoughtfulness and flattery. Which reminds me

of the husband who brought home some candy for no other reason than just to be nice, only to be met with a suspicious snarl, "Now what are you up to?" Sort of takes the joy out of candy buying, doesn't it?

Boaz was a no-nonsense individual. When he had a task to do, it got done. He didn't dilly-dally around, putting important things off. He was a man of action: decisive, thorough, considerate, kind, gentle, and generous—all the ingredients necessary for a good marriage, but also the ingredients that can destroy a marriage. For the bad often take advantage of the good . . . the weak of the strong.

Most marriages don't thrive too well when a hard-working, ambitious woman is mated to a lazy, thoughtless, inconsiderate, milquetoast husband. But when you put an ambitious, hard-working, devoted woman like Ruth into a yoke with a man like Boaz, it has to work out. Which leads us to Ruth.

## RUTH

Ruth was a widow, possibly somewhat younger than Boaz. She was as loyal as a woman can get. She was willing to forsake her country, her kinsmen, and her childhood and youthful gods—with no guarantee of anything in return. She had no idea that Boaz existed; that she would fall into the lineage of Jesus Christ, the promised Messiah; that her poverty would be short lived. She probably had already resigned

85

herself to living the life of a destitute widow, dutifully and lovingly supporting her beloved mother-in-law.

Ruth was energetic and ambitious. She impressed Boaz, not only because of her presence but because of her dedication. She didn't try to flirt with the men around her or seek to gain favors. With all these virtues—and more—her marriage was determined to succeed. She was loyal, ambitious, discreet, appreciative, and godly. What a wonderful discovery for both Ruth and Boaz when providentially they were brought together into one family.

## THAT ETERNAL TRIANGLE

A third party or passion can easily rock the ship called matrimony. Both Ruth and Boaz were people of high ideals and dedication. They were both extremely capable individuals, no-nonsense oriented, ambitious, poised, and self-reliant. Any of these virtues—to say nothing of all of them together—could spell disaster for a marriage when both parties are more or less equally endowed. Ruth and Boaz survived this potential ordeal, not because one became subservient to the other (which doubtless was true to a certain extent, particularly in that culture) but because they, as individuals, rose above their virtues. Their abilities and personalities were not more important than their marriage.

There were other potential hazards that they escaped as well. Both were proud people. Boaz

could have frustrated their situation quite easily by refusing to accept his responsibility as kinsman. Ruth could have refused to do that strange thing Naomi suggested about lying at his feet in the middle of the night in a barn full of men. Both, however, refused to let anything daunt them from doing what was right. These were not two stubborn-but-well-endowed fools.

They were both leaders, ambitious, perhaps even aggressive (remember, Boaz was more than just a one-man operation). They could have clashed easily but they didn't. When Ruth asked permission to glean, it was granted. When Boaz offered her a shawl full of grain, she thanked him. No superiority or inferiority—just two people who recognized that being a person is much superior to lauding a virtue or languishing in a vice. Ruth and Boaz were well matched—even though he was a landed gentleman and she was a peasant, he was well-to-do and she was destitute, he was held in high regard and she was a foreigner. To Ruth and Boaz it made no difference.

We have seen that either the possession of virtues or the lack of them can cause a marriage to crumble. Couples can be too compatible just as they can be incompatible. But there is something begging for a comment here: the third party. This can be a man or a woman—competitors or villains, lonely people or starving creatures. All are capable of destruction. There is another third party also in the story of Ruth and Boaz: an in-law. When an in-law becomes the apex of a triangle, look out.

I've often wondered what happened to Boaz' mother. She is not mentioned and it could be presumed that she was not around. If not, Ruth would have had two mothers-in-law—which could have been an interesting situation.

The account tells us that there was Ruth, Boaz, Naomi; and then a son was born. The triangle became a quadrangle. And so what happened? Naomi, related to baby Obed through her husband and as mother-in-law to the mother of the child, became the infant's nurse—a built-in baby sitter. This can be a blessing and it can be a curse. To further complicate the situation, Naomi, as a proud grandmother, showed the little fellow off to her neighbors. They immediately suggested a name, and so the child was named.

Apart from any cultural peculiarity, the potential for disaster was ripe. However, something else saved the day. Naomi, seasoned and sobered by the passing of time, didn't change her character or her personality. She was a woman of loyalty, generosity, love, thoughtfulness, and dignity. It appears reasonably safe to assume that she did what all in-laws are supposed to do: add to marriage and childbirth, not take away from it.

*Ruth and Boaz were well matched. It seemed to run in the family.*

1. In-laws have been a blessing and a curse as long as they have existed. Describe, from your own experience, some good examples of in-law relationships; describe some unfortunate experiences. (Be discreet: use anonymous situations, etc.)

2. How would you describe and explain the different responses between Naomi and her two daughters-in-law?
3. What is the proper role of an in-law? On whom is the burden to keep peace in the family: the older or younger person? both? a third party?
4. How can a person give "more than sympathy" in sorrow and tragedy? What can a Christian give that a non-Christian cannot?
5. The idea of the Biblical kinsman's responsibility in family life has diminished considerably in Western culture. Would it work today? Was there actually something universal about the kinsman idea? What about the manner of giving relief (welfare); Can we learn anything from Ruth's gleaning experience and the laws of the land?
6. What was meant when it was said the very ingredients that cause a marriage to fall apart are the same ones that make a marriage successful? Do you agree?
7. Ruth, Boaz, and Naomi were well-matched, mature, godly people. Does this kind of character run in the family? Does maturity beget maturity? Do lightweight Christians beget lightweight Christians?

READING FURTHER . . .

The Book of Ruth

A CASE STUDY . . .

Bill and Judy, with the help of a third party, solved their marital hassle and ended the game they were playing, only to inherit another difficulty. Their eldest daughter, Peg, had married, creating an unfortunate in-law situation. Bill and Peg's husband couldn't seem to get along. Bill was resentful of Peg's marriage and was disappointed in her choice. Judy had to be the peacemaker, which drove a wedge between Bill and herself. WHAT COULD JUDY DO WITHOUT RISKING HER OWN MARRIAGE? WHERE WAS HER FIRST LOYALTY? HOW DOES THEIR CHRISTIAN FAITH ENTER THE PICTURE (THEY ARE ALL BELIEVERS)?

# 8

# DAVID AND BATHSHEBA

## On Being Married to a King

*Bathsheba bowed low to the king and prostrated herself; and she said, "May my lord King David live for ever!"*

I Kings 1:31

It's one thing to dream of marrying a king; it's something else to be married to one.

Being married to a great man has both its rewards and penalties, its ups and downs, its ecstasies and anguish. The greater the man, the greater the marriage ought to be. But often it isn't! Kings and other important people are at best inconsistent like most people, except their strengths and weaknesses are usually more pronounced. A king might be a great warrior but a lousy husband. He might have a heart of gold but spoil his kids rotten. He might be an ace-high statesman in the palace but a two-bit politician at home.

David, like most great men, was far from perfect. Bathsheba, a beautiful though ordinary

woman, was equally far from imperfect. The two managed to merge somewhere between their perfections and imperfections. Which makes for a pretty good marriage.

## AVOIDING THE EXTREMES

One danger in marriage is to worship the ground on which your spouse walks. When a wife does this she is often treated like dirt. It is not healthy to be so wrapped up in your husband that he can do no evil in the sight of God or man. Even though the clinging vine little woman can be a pleasant companion, she can also become a suffocating burden. She wrecks her own life and spoils her husband in the process.

On the other hand, a woman can take that same ground she used to worship and throw it at her husband. Some even add a little water to it. Many husbands would never taste mud were it not for their wives.

Now, let's face it. It usually doesn't hurt a husband to have his wife clobber him with a clod of dirt now and then. It's usually much safer than a rock and accomplishes the same purpose. But to worship the ground he walks on or constantly throw mud at him is just too unaccommodating. A husband deserves better treatment.

Whether you're a queen or a peasant, you must seek to walk that narrow pathway between spoiling him rotten on one hand and smashing

his ego on the other. Perhaps it's not quite as important to keep on that difficult path all the time as it is knowing there is such a path. Many women have never hit that trail.

Bathsheba—we have good reason to believe—was quite aware of her awesome roles as the wife of a man as well as the queen to a king.

## ON FINDING YOUR NEW ROLE

Bathsheba had quite an adjustment to make. She became David's wife only to be ushered into an expanding harem. This not only took a certain amount of grace but a lot of nerve. She had had an affair with the king while her husband was out fighting his battle. She was lonely and was terribly flattered when David sent for her. She became pregnant during their first affair. David tried to cover it up by sending for her husband. But friend husband was suspicious and refused to see his wife. This frustrated David, which prompted him to send him back into the thick of battle where he would most certainly be killed. He was.

When David married her, her adjustment was further complicated because David had a couple of sons who were, to put it bluntly, spoiled brats. How they responded to their pregnant stepmother is not hard to guess. Besides, it was far more romantic to make love with the king before they were married than to take turns sleeping with him after the ceremony. Her adjustment to her new role as queen and wife and

mother and stepmother was not an easy one. It was even more difficult to become just another one of his several wives.

Our marital adjustments are usually not this complicated, but they are still major adjustments and readjustments. If they aren't, we're probably taking our vows too lightly. On the other hand, God has decreed that when a man and a woman commit themselves to each other, they become one. Contrary to the understanding of many, God never intended for man to share more than one woman. This was man's doing (and his undoing). Just because the patriarchs and the kings married many times does not mean that this was God's plan for mankind. Once it was done, it took a long time for God's people to get back to the monogamous ideal. We face the same danger in our culture, which glories not so much in a polygamous marriage as in an easy succession of marriages. Western civilization may seldom see the ideal marriage again, when vows are made "until death us do part"— when two become one in body and soul, for richer or poorer, in health and in sorrow. . . .

## HOW COMPLICATED CAN IT GET?

Bathsheba, had she known what she was getting into, might have wished she had drawn the curtains when she bathed. Marriage often is a strange relationship. Although the original idea was conceived in heaven, marriages at best are rather earthy. A man and a woman must retain

93

their own individual integrity while blending their lives into one. Marriage to big shots can be disastrous (and when two big shots get married, look out!—Hollywood and Wall Street and General Hospital can testify to this).

Men can and do outgrow their britches. When a man stretches and reaches high up the ladder, his life is bound to be much more complicated than that of the man who is content to sit on one of the bottom rungs. It can be, however, much more rewarding to wrestle with a tycoon than to cuddle with a teddy bear. But to each his own.

David was a big shot. He was complicated, exasperating, quarrelsome and tenderhearted, magnanimous and petty, handsome and talented and wealthy and powerful. This is rough on matrimony. This kind of a man is tough to be married to. This is what Bathsheba inherited when she consented to be his wife, or we should say, one of his wives. She probably knew quite a bit about the king before she married him (but no one really knows the person they marry—just the marriage itself changes people overnight). But being the wife of a public servant, Bathsheba probably knew much of the general knowledge about David and some of the private information, gossip, and otherwise.

She certainly would know about Adonijah, Ammon, and Absalom, David's troublesome sons. She probably also knew that he had to kneel beside a tiny casket which nearly broke his tender heart. She had to know about Michal,

Saul's daughter who was given to David in a rather sordid deal. Saul offered David his daughter in exchange for one hundred Philistines. David, proud and profane, doubled that insidious order, knowing good and well that Saul intended that David would get killed in the process. She also must have known that David could have murdered Saul several times but refused to touch God's anointed. Bathsheba probably realized that David was far too complex for a simple woman like Michal. Michal was terribly upset with David, a man who could act in great dignity one moment and clown like a buffoon the next.

David had just triumphed over the Philistines with a smashing victory. He returned to Jerusalem with the ark of the covenant, restoring it to its rightful place. The victory was being celebrated with delirious shouts and songs and dancing. King David went crazy, leaping madly before the crowd as he led the victory parade. Michal watched this breach of dignity in horror; and when David came home, she cut him down by telling him what a fool he had made of himself.

David was stung, and he retaliated by telling her that he'd keep right on dancing before the Lord who had chosen him instead of her father. Ouch! They hurt each other. Badly. Permanently. As far as we know, that was the end of their intimacy. Michal, Saul's daughter, had no child to her dying day.

Bathsheba, on the other hand, understood the crazy, mixed-up enigma she had married, and

emerged as the one who wept and laughed and brooded over her king who was also her husband. If it is true that behind every great man there is a great woman, Bathsheba is her name.

## GREAT MEN CAN DO STUPID THINGS

All men everywhere make mistakes. Some are deliberate; others result from preoccupation or busyness or indifference or carelessness or just plain stupidity. David, a fearless warrior, was also a man with a compassionate and forgiving heart; he could laugh and weep and sing and shout and whisper; he was a man who could love and kill and forgive and forget; he could sing and dance and play; he could pen a psalm or compose a song or dictate an edict; he was a man good to look at, at home in the fields or in the city; he could curse and pray, almost in the same breath; and he was a man who could weep and did weep for his sins. He was as stupid and foolish as he was wise and brilliant.

When we think of what he did to Bathsheba that fateful afternoon, we shudder. Now we shudder to think of what David might have been without her.

Among the many idiotic things he did, one of the worst legacies he left behind was his example of how not to raise children. He was a lousy father.

David grew a large family but he was unprepared to handle it. He wasn't adequately equipped

to handle the newly acquired wealth of the expanding kingdom. The princes and princesses grew up in an environment woefully lacking in paternal discipline. They were extravagantly indulged; and though they often tortured the soul of their father and brought his wrath down on them, David never really lowered the boom. Not even when Ammon, one of his sons, seduced his half sister Tamar.

Ammon pretended to be ill, and when Tamar came into his room to wait on him, he threw back the covers and made her lie with him. Her protests and pleading did her no good. When he was through with her, his lust turned into disgust and he drove her out of his sight. What did King David do? Nothing. Ammon fled but David did nothing.

Absalom, however, did. He was Tamar's full-blooded brother. Seething with anger, he bided his time. After awhile he avenged this dastardly deed by killing his half brother and then fled, remaining in seclusion until the memory began to grow dim.

David, as with so many fathers, was torn between the bitter, perverse anguish he felt toward his son and his intense love and loyalty. Absalom eventually returned home, only to continue to nourish his lust for his father's throne. He began by winning over the people with his charm and smooth manners. Then he began, very cleverly, to assume certain prerogatives that belonged only to the king. As he realized his

97

power, and saw that he had developed quite a following, he felt that at last he had successfully divided the loyalties. So did the king.

In fact, Absalom had won over the closest advisors to the king—his right-hand men. But David didn't want to believe that his son would do this to him. By now he realized that Absalom could do it. Absalom, convinced that the time was ripe, made plans to seize the kingdom by force. So, what did King David do? He fled rather than stand up to his rebellious son. Eventually David had to crush the insurrection; and when he did, Absalom fled for his life. As he tried to escape, Absalom's unusually long hair got caught in the boughs of a tree, and there he hung until David's general put a dart through his heart.

This was in direct violation of David's orders to his men to go easy on his son. When he heard the news, David wept bitterly for Absalom. In fact, he became so despondent he wanted to die. Finally his general, Joab, jolted David out of his depression and David began to act like the king that he was.

There will always be the struggle between doing what is right against doing what is the most satisfying at the moment. David let his kids get away with murder and they nearly murdered him. Bathsheba actually inherited a family when she became queen. These treacherous deeds were done, not by her children, but by David's sons, her stepsons. Although there is no proof for this, it appears that thanks to Bathsheba, David re-

arranged some of his child-rearing prejudices under her ministrations.

Why men in high places so often make mistakes at home that would never occur in the office remains one of the bitter mysteries of life. Being the wife and mother to a great man (or a big shot) is no easy task. Blessed is the man who is married to one of these gems. Her presence at his side is worth far more than a sudden surge in the stock market. And blessed is the woman whose man knows this!

## PROFESSIONAL JEALOUSY

In concluding this very myopic view of David and Bathsheba, there is a final episode which took place at the end of David's life that must not be overlooked. Here, let Scripture tell the story: "King David was now a very old man and, though they wrapped clothes around him, he could not keep warm. So his household said to him, 'Let us find a young virgin for your majesty, to attend you and take care of you; and let her lie in your bosom, sir, and make you warm.' So they searched all over Israel for a beautiful maiden and found Abishag, a Shunammite, and brought her to the king. She was a very beautiful girl, and she took care of the king and waited on him, but he had no intercourse with her" (I Kings 1:1-4).

At this precise time, Bathsheba heard the bad news that another of her stepsons, Adonijah, was plotting to steal the kingdom away from his

99

aged father. He too was a spoiled, cunning, smooth operator. He too was able to win over the confidants of the king and they conspired together against David. Nathan, the prophet, urged Bathsheba to go to David and remind him of the promise he had made long ago when he swore to Bathsheba that her son, Solomon, was to succeed him on the throne.

The queen did go to the king who responded, "What do you want?" David's wife, the mother of his son Solomon, with the seasoned maturity of many years of living in close proximity to the throne, bowed low and spoke softly: "My lord, you swore to me your servant, by the Lord your God, that my son Solomon would succeed you as king, and that he should sit on your throne. But now, here is Adonijah, all unknown to your majesty. He has sacrificed great numbers of oxen, buffaloes, and sheep, and has invited to the feast all the king's sons, and Abiathar the priest, but he has not invited your servant Solomon. And now, your majesty, all Israel is looking to you to announce who is to succeed you on the throne. Otherwise, when you, sir, rest with your forefathers, my son Solomon and I shall be treated as criminals" (I Kings 1:16-21). Bathsheba entered the presence of the king with great respect and a deep concern. She knew that Adonijah was not worthy of the throne; and she also knew that if he ascended, Solomon would probably die. And she would too. It might be tempting to say that she only cared enough to

see her flesh and blood anointed and her life spared. It could be, but it is doubtful; and I would think she has earned the benefit of a doubt.

No woman enjoys stepping aside while another waits on her husband. Indeed, she could very well have been a vital part of the household which suggested this unusual disposition to bring warmth to a man waiting for the chilly hands of death. Her graciousness and her tone of voice tell us something important about a woman who could have been bitter with anxiety and jealous of the beautiful woman who had taken her place in his bosom.

It is extremely difficult for a woman not to become jealous (or envious) of her husband, especially if he is a king and she has to linger in the shadows of the throne. A great man's life is full of awe and wonder, excitement and adventure. He gets to go where the action is—to new places—with important and interesting people—while she stays at home and changes diapers and slugs it out at the PTA. Big deals are always happening; and while he gets to go on a corporate safari to London, she trucks off to the laundromat.

Yes, let's face it. It is quite natural for the little woman to become just a wee bit jealous or resentful at times. This can be compounded by the cute little secretary who thinks the boss is king and becomes more than a little possessive. Sooner or later there is the danger of the atmo-

sphere between husband and wife (king and queen) becoming a bit chilly. In fact, in time it could freeze.

Bathsheba lived in this kind of turmoil and weathered it admirably. She had learned the delicate art of living with a mortal man who was also a king.

1. Explain: "It's one thing to dream of marrying a king; it's something else to be married to one." How else could we define *king* in our everyday life today?
2. What is the danger of "worshiping the ground on which your spouse walks"? Can a woman *love* a man too much? Can a man *love* a woman too much?
3. What kind of adjustments did Bathsheba have to make? Is this a difference in kind or degree compared with our marital adjustments today? What are some of the adjustments you had to make when you got married? Are you still adjusting?
4. What are some of the problems of being married to an important person? What makes a person truly great? Is it true that behind every great man there is a great woman (his mother? wife? another?)?
5. David had many wives and concubines delineated in the Old Testament. Does this mean that God *approved* or *tolerated* this dimension of David's life? Why did God bless the union of David and Bathsheba despite the circumstances? What does this tell us of God? of David? of Bathsheba?
6. Why was Bathsheba so successful, so gracious, so merciful in spite of such adverse circumstances?
7. How much tension is good for a marriage? When does it become harmful? How could such a rascal as David also be such a godly man?

READING FURTHER . . .

I Samuel 16—II Samuel 24; I Kings 1; Psalm 23, 103, 139

A CASE STUDY . . .

It finally happened. The estrangement between Judy and Bill widened until it ended in divorce. Judy did not dream of remarrying; but one day she met a handsome widower, fell in love, and they were married. He simultaneously inherited a built-in family, including Peg and Norm (Judy's daughter and husband plus two children) besides Judy's other children still at home. Judy's new husband had three children. Judy is quite happy in her new situation but life is terribly hectic. Her way of raising children is obviously different than his. She now is nearly frantic and has called on you for help. WHAT WOULD YOU DO? HOW WOULD YOU ADVISE HER? (Note: YOU ADVISED HER NOT TO REMARRY BUT SHE DID SO ANYWAY. WHAT IS YOUR RESPONSIBILITY NOW?)

# 9

# HOSEA AND GOMER

## The Decline and Fall of a Marriage

*I will block her road with thorn-bushes and obstruct her path with a wall, so that she can no longer follow her old ways.*

Hosea 2:6

The story of Hosea and Gomer is one of the most amazing pieces of literature in the Bible. It is also one of the most tender but pathetic love stories ever written.

Most scholars consider the story an allegory and we will do the same. However, let us think of Hosea and Gomer as real people. Then we won't have to shift our thinking back and forth between allegory and reality, fantasy and the unromantic.

### SHE'S DOUBLY MINE

Remember that touching little story of the lad who made a toy sailboat but lost it during its maiden voyage? He was terribly upset until one

day when he spied his boat in a shop keeper's window with a FOR SALE sign on it. Quickly he went in and claimed the boat he knew belonged to him. The merchant was unmoved and sent the boy on his bitter way. Suddenly, a brilliant thought crossed his young mind. He quickly began to earn a few pennies here and there until he had enough to buy his boat back. Rushing off to the pawn shop, he laid the cash on the counter, wrapped his arms around the homemade sailboat, and sighed, "Now you're doubly mine; first I made you, now I bought you."

This in a nutshell is the story of the Book of Hosea. Hosea was married to an incorrigible prostitute. No matter what he did, she kept going back to her paramours. Her husband, brokenhearted but forgiving, kept trying to restore his wayward wife to himself. His hope never dimmed, and eventually he got her back for fifteen pieces of silver, a homer of barley, and a measure of wine. He brought her back home and kept her in his house, this time refusing to allow her to leave. She was now not only his wife but also his property. Legally, she could no longer leave him to do her own thing. First he married her; then he bought her.

Incredible? Unbelievable? No woman could be this rotten and no man could be this forgiving. Or can they? If we knew the whole truth, husbands and wives everywhere, yesterday and today, have forgiven (but perhaps not forgotten) some incredible sins. Husbands have harbored

mistresses and cheated innocent wives who remained faithful and loving through it all. And husbands have held their homes together while their wives went awhoring. Yes, these are exceptions, not the rule. Many marriages have crumbled for considerably lesser reasons.

This is the story of Hosea and Gomer, amazing but believable.

## A MAN WITH A BROKEN HEART

Hosea was a magnificent person. He was a godly man, a true prophet, the only author to come out of the Northern Kingdom of Israel. His prophetic insight was uncanny, predicting the decline and fall of the kingdom with bold and devastating accuracy. He lived in Israel during the regime of five kings, at a time when the nation was undergoing a period of national turbulence. As we attempt to understand the political, economic, and spiritual climate of this era, we are amazed at the parallel between his times and those of today.

Hosea lived in a time of great prosperity. The Northern Kingdom was marked by a high degree of economic and commercial development. Urban life had attracted many people from agricultural regions, causing the cities to mushroom. This mobility also caused some severe problems.

A strong middle class arose, forcing abrupt changes in a country which had known only two classes: the very rich and the poor. The increasingly impoverished small farmers were forced

into selling out and moved into the cities to find work. The whole nation was in a turmoil but never had a chance to straighten itself out.

The Israelites had intermingled and inter-married with the pagan Canaanites and had com-promised their religious practices. The corrupt, abominable rites of the pagan rituals had already gained a stranglehold on the Hebrews. They were rapidly abandoning the Jehovah of their fathers as they lusted after Baal, the male fertili-ty god, and Ashtoreth, the savage, sensuous fe-male deity. The religious ceremonies, practiced several times a year, were characterized by drunkenness, acts of violence and prostitution.

The religious life of the people of Israel had degenerated beyond imagination. Alcohol ran freely, threatening both the Canaanites as well as the people of the Northern tribes. To make a lengthy tale short, the nation was crumbling because of materialism, secularism, and a declin-ing moral vitality. Hosea spoke out against this abomination, finally resorting to the powerful message found in the book that bears his name. Israel was likened to Gomer, a hopeless prosti-tute, and the Lord God was likened to her faithful husband, Hosea. This audacity probably shocked the people, but Hosea was desperate. He had to get through to his people somehow. This shocked them into sobriety, but it wasn't enough. Israel ignored Hosea's warning and his passionate pleading, continuing toward an inevi-table destruction. Hosea never lost hope but must have died with a broken heart.

# HANKY-PANKY CAN BE HABIT FORMING

If we look carefully, we'll discover several amazing insights into reasons why marriages crumble. Hosea more than suggests that fooling around with the ideals of marriage can become habit forming. Gomer would stay home for awhile and then head out for greener pastures, where her lovers took good care of her (so she said). Then she would come home again, only to take off on another pilgrimage. During the earlier years of their marriage, three children were born to them, which suggests a certain amount of stability in their relationship (although many children are born under horribly unstable marital relationships). Gomer's hanky-panky did become habit forming; and Hosea, a great man and a godly person, was unable to do much about it. Finally, Hosea had an opportunity. He discovered where she was. She had fallen so deeply into prostitution that she had presumably become the chattel of another man or possibly a slave in a brothel. In either case, for a price, Hosea was able to purchase her freedom—which he did. He then took her back home—for good this time.

Marital faithfulness—in spite of all the fads to the contrary—is infinitely superior to the ignoble vice of unfaithfulness (even if for awhile it's a lot of fun). In spite of the cultural condoning of wife swapping and lesser hanky-panky, the ultimate repercussions are nothing compared to the danger of cultivating a practice which can easily become habit forming. The titillating thrill of a

clandestine rendezvous at a cheap motel is one thing; it's quite another to keep up the practice.

## THE CULTURAL SHOCK

Hosea has a very creative way of reminding us that it's usually rough to shrug off our environment. Marriages often crumble, not so much due to incompatibilities between two people as an incompatibility between a couple and the culture around them. So many marriages seem destined for near perfection on that lovely Saturday afternoon when the vows are purred with an innocent idealism. And nothing foreign really comes along to mar the marriage, but still it declines and dies. Why? Because it was rocked by the after-waves of a cultural shock.

Terry and Toni were an ideal couple if ever such a couple existed. Their marriage was a noble one: good upbringing, well suited for each other with reasonably similar interests and disinterests (these are important too!), plus a strong personal faith in God and in their fellow man. What they didn't realize was inevitable (but no one told them—and if they were told, they weren't listening): life can get pretty rough at times.

Terry had a good job and was next in line for a handsome promotion, but it was given to a nobody from an alien department. Terry took it pretty well, but his scrumptious little secretary was incensed. Before long she had embittered her boss against the company and so he found

solace in her well-intended (at first) sympathies. These soon led to a mini affair which leaked through the corporate underground until it reached Toni, who caught the next bus for her mother. Time healed this injury and Terry fired his scrumptious little secretary, but they didn't live happily ever after.

Toni, after waiting so long, had her hopes dashed when she suffered a miscarriage. Terry, who tried so hard to be sympathetic, only made the situation worse. A busybody next door told them that this was an ill omen and that God was punishing them for their ungodliness. This made Terry furious and he refused to attend church from that day onward. Shortly after, their car was sideswiped while they were sound asleep and a mysterious disease destroyed their entire lawn.

Then, alas—Terrance lost his job and Toni discovered that she was pregnant again. Only this time she resented it. Then Toni's father had a heart attack which nearly took his life, leaving him a semi-invalid.

Meanwhile, Toni and Terry had begun to travel with some couples in their neighborhood who had become enamored with astrology. They read the daily horoscope and gradually discovered to their horror they were indeed hooked! They actually lived in fear of the daily column. The cocktail parties with friends had now become a regular occurrence at home. Whereas it had been *tea for two*, it was now a *martini or two*. Through it all they clung to each other all the

harder. Their marriage, they thought, was being strengthened as the world closed in on them.

Then came the crusher. Their parties with the couples were running out of ideas. The astrology kick and the alcohol were now mere habits—they were no longer hot stuff. Something new was emerging, but they hardly realized it until it reared its ugly head. Gradually they had gotten so friendly with each other that previously forbidden liberties had become commonplace. They had actually swapped partners without knowing it. Their affections had subtly switched back and forth until they were psychologically swapping mates, not exactly like the couples in Updike's New England town, but enough to shatter faith in each other. If suspicions could kill, they would all be dead.

Before it was over, Terry and Toni put it all back together again; but, like Humpty Dumpty, there were some ugly cracks in the shell which never quite disappeared. Terry and Toni were victims of a brutal cultural shock. They couldn't handle it because, like the Israelites in the time of Hosea and Gomer, they had surrendered their faith in the living God for a materialistic and secularistic alliance with a foreign god.

The decline and fall of many marriages often has far less to do with falling out of love than with knuckling under to society. Gomer was a victim of her environment and became a slave to it. Hosea remained true to his God and his convictions and saved his wife from her enslavement—but not without an awful price.

## TOO SOON WE GET OLD
## AND TOO LATE SMART

We've all smiled at this injunction in its various forms. Hosea finally got smart! When he discovered that his wanton wife had sold herself into a horrible slavery, he finally took action that stopped all this nonsense once and for all.

We marvel at the patience and compassion of this man who never gave up, who kept on looking for his stubborn, sinful wife and brought her back home—not once, but many times. How many times should a husband forgive his wife (or a wife her husband)? Once? Twice? The pointed story is oft told about the old timer who had just married a wife. As they were riding in his wagon, the horse balked and the man whipped it mercilessly, shouting, "That's once!" His wife just looked on in horror. A short time later, the horse balked again. Once more the husband whipped the poor thing with no pity and screamed, "That's twice!!" They kept on going when again the poor horse faltered. This time the man whipped out his gun and shot the creature.

The poor bride gasped in horror, "Dear, do you think you should have done that?" Turning on the poor woman, he bellowed, "That's once!" The story, with its crude humor, does make quite a forceful point.

When a marriage sours, what do we do? How long do we forgive and forget (if we can)? How many times must we walk the second mile? seventy times? seventy times seven?

Hosea, realizing that he could get his wife back, not simply by claiming her, but by actually buying back stolen property, did just that. By paying for her, he gave his beloved her freedom from prostitution by making her both his wife and his slave. While she was only his wife, she could leave him and seek out her lovers; but now that she was his slave, she could not leave him. He finally put a stop to her wanton behavior. He not only forgave her, but he restored her to her rightful place in his home although there were restrictions placed on their relationship.

Once, in my ministry, I was plagued by an individual who kept annoying me with senseless telephone calls and unnecessary visits. At times I was pestered several times a day. One day I finally wised up. When another call came, telling me off and indicting my congregation as well, I refused to answer. I simply stayed on the line but said not a word. Pretty soon there were a few mumbled words damning me for hanging up. A couple days later I received a resignation via telegram (which was later regretted but we had already ignored it). This ended this marathon nonsense and paved the way for some serious talk regarding a responsible role in life.

This thing of forgiving the same sins over and over again might be just as wrong as not forgiving. When we see a marriage beginning to decline, we don't have the right to watch it decline until it falls. It is infinitely better to do something about it even though it can be dreadfully painful. This goes for our own marriages as well as those of our neighbors.

It must have grieved Hosea something terribly to watch his wife turn into a hardened, brazen, diabolical bitch (even though she was a wanton woman to begin with); but it probably hurt even more to bring her home for the last time, especially when the odds of her restoration were so overwhelmingly against her. Even though Hosea never gave up hope for Israel, his beloved country, it went into a tailspin and never stopped until it crashed. And that was the end of the Northern Kingdom.

## IN CONCLUSION

The Book of Hosea could well be only an allegory of the love of the Lord God. for a wayward, rebellious people. But it is also a moving story of a man who loved his wayward wife so much that he refused to give up hope. How easily do we give up hope? How soon do we quit loving? When does our forgiveness do more harm than good—or isn't this ever possible?

Hosea and Gomer are rare people in the history of matrimony. We should be eternally thankful that our forefathers so long ago included this unique book in the canon of sacred writ. Without it we might forget some very essential things such as:

*hanky-panky in marriage can be habit forming;
the world around us can quite easily squeeze the spiritual strength right out of us;*
and, *we can give up too easily and forgive too readily, strange as it may seem.*

1. In our culture we seem to think of the man as the unfaithful partner in most situations. In this situation, the wife was the wayward one. Why is it that prostitution and having a mistress are so much a part of history?
2. Is the sin of Gomer believable? then? today? Is the compassion of Hosea believable? Explain: hanky-panky can be habit forming.
3. What happens when a believer marries an unbeliever? What are the odds against success? What are the odds in favor of the believer seeing the unbelieving partner become a believer?
4. Was the waywardness of Gomer a sudden or a gradual thing? Could this happen to anyone? Why did she keep going back to her paramours?
5. Do you agree that incompatibility with life is more detrimental to a marriage than incompatibility between a husband and his wife? Explain.
6. In what way is Hosea a type of God? of Christ? of a godly husband?
7. When a marriage is declining, is there a danger of giving up too easily? of being too forgiving for too long? Elaborate on Hosea 2:6.

FOR FURTHER READING . . .

The Book of Hosea; Hebrews 13:4; I Corinthians 7:10-16

A CASE STUDY . . .

Judy and Tom, her new husband, managed quite well for awhile. But Judy, very attractive, burdened by a certain amount of guilt and shame, enjoyed the attention she received at work. She began subtly to encourage these men and before too long she had a couple of so-called harmless affairs going. Tom was on the road quite a bit, which made it both lonely for Judy as well as convenient. One day he returned from a trip a day earlier than expected, walked into his own home only to discover his unfaithful wife in the arms of another man. TOM SAID NOT A WORD BUT WALKED OUT OF THE HOUSE

AND WENT TO A MOTEL. YOU ARE CLOSE
FRIENDS TO THE FAMILY AND WANT TO SAL-
VAGE THIS MARRIAGE IF YOU CAN. HOW WOULD
YOU GO ABOUT IT?

# 10

# ESTHER AND XERXES

## The Myth of Incompatibility

*The king loved her more than any of his other women and treated her with greater favor and kindness than the rest. . . .*

Esther 2:17

Esther was a beautiful foreign woman who won one of the world's first beauty contests. The king of Persia had divorced his wife (or had an annulment; she had defied his drunken orders), and so he was advised to hold a contest as a sporting way to find a suitable replacement.

King Ahasuerus wasn't quite prepared for this charming Jewish orphan by the name of Hadassah. (Her name was then changed to Esther, which meant "star." The reason for changing it was to conceal her national identity.) Esther charmed everyone in sight, and not only won the beauty contest hands down but took first honors as the girl most likely to succeed as well as the Miss Congeniality of her day.

## WHO IS THIS KING AHASUERUS?

The word *ahasuerus* is probably a title similar to *caesar* or *pharaoh* rather than the name of a particular man. It is generally thought that the actual king was Xerxes, and so we'll assume that it is. The title means "high father" or ruler, and someone has said that it is mentioned 192 times in one of the versions of this short but delightful story. The setting takes place somewhere around the early part of the fifth century B.C. and is another one of the marvelous contributions to literary history found only in the Bible.

Xerxes was a Persian king who took a shot at world dominion and fell short. In order to get psyched up for his conquest, he prepared a banquet which lasted for 180 days! Unfortunately, by the seventh day he was somewhat inebriated, and in a weak moment commanded Queen Vashti to appear so that the men could look her over (only men attended this affair). The queen balked, refusing to obey the king.

This put the poor man in a bind. What if word would ever get out that the queen defied the king's orders? This would not only be embarrassing but could cause horrible repercussions in the ranks. After mulling it over, the king decided to annul the marriage (foreshadow of Henry VIII). This he did; and according to the infamous law of the Medes and Persians, his action was irreversible.

Then King Ahasuerus moved against Greece but lost decisively. His entire fleet was destroyed in the Aegean; so he, in his madness, beat the

waves of the sea with a strop, taking his revenge out on the waters which had risen against him. Xerxes, like so many military leaders (like Napoleon and Hitler), was a complex figure, partly mad but perhaps mostly eccentric.

With his big dream shattered, he hoped to forget the ordeal by indulging in excesses. He would have enjoyed the comfort of Queen Vashti at this time, but he had already shoved her off into the past. No doubt he regretted his rash behavior but it was the law—his law—and he had to live up to it. What a pity! But men do it all the time. Why is it so difficult to admit making a mistake? Ask Xerxes.

It was in this mood that the king's servants suggested having a beauty contest as a novel way to have a little fun while getting over the mood of despondency. Besides, it would solve many problems in selecting a suitable queen as a replacement of the banished wife. Xerxes agreed and preparations were begun.

## A PERSIAN BEAUTY CONTEST

Our Miss America and other contests might be a bit pale compared to this one. If a king could throw a banquet lasting half a year, imagine what he could do with a beauty contest. A year was set aside for the contest, and what a year it was. Commissioners were appointed in all the provinces to seek out beautiful young women. They were then brought to the summer palace of Shushan (Susa).

Esther had been adopted by her uncle, a man

by the name of Mordecai, the great-grandson of Kish, a Benjamite who had been carried captive to Persia many years earlier. She was a Jewess but so far removed from her ancestors that no one really knew her background. Mordecai, knowing well that her charm and beauty would go a long way, made sure that one of those commissioners discovered her. He also cautioned her against revealing her background. She was therefore added to the growing number of gorgeous contestants.

She was brought to the palace with the other beautiful women, where they underwent a year of preparation. Esther attracted the attention of the attendant and received his special favor. He provided her with the necessary cosmetics, her allowance of food, and also picked seven carefully chosen maids from the king's palace. Besides, he gave her and her maids special privileges in the women's quarters. For six months they were prepared with oil and myrrh and six months with perfumes and cosmetics.

The day came for the contest and Esther, with her inner beauty as well as physical grace, walked away with the crown: "When she was taken to King Ahasuerus in the royal palace ... the king loved her more than any of his other women. ... He put a crown on her head and made her queen in place of Vashti."[1]

---

[1] Some Biblical scholars are troubled by historical accounts which fail to mention Esther (or Hadassah), claiming that Amestris became queen in the third year of Xerxes' reign and ruled after his death. This could be

Trouble began almost instantly. Haman was promoted as chief officer, which meant that everyone but the king had to bow when he passed by. Mordecai, because of his Jewish heritage, refused to bow to any man, including Haman. This infuriated the chief officer, who began to look desperately for a way to retaliate. Somehow he found out that Mordecai was a Jew, an alien; and he knew that Jews were scattered throughout the kingdom. A devilish scheme was conceived, and Haman went to Xerxes with a trumped-up charge that a bunch of aliens living in the land were violating the king's laws. He poured it on thick, with the result that the eccentric king became furious, ordering the destruction of every Jew in every province.

What Xerxes didn't know—nor did Haman—was about to hurt him. He, the king, was unwittingly married to a Jewess but had now signed a proclamation that would mean her death. He could not retract his word. It was law, the law of the Medes and Persians. This often happens when we act in anger or fail to get all the facts. Xerxes did both, besides trusting in a man who couldn't be trusted. Any man with such a lust for power cannot possibly be all heart.

---

correct, particularly if the Book of Esther is fictional. However, it is also quite probable that Esther was a secondary wife, favored and honored, but unknown to historians.

Now, let's face it! Xerxes didn't do his homework. How many tragic deeds have been done because people didn't do their homework we'll never be able to tally. How many marriages have flunked because someone didn't do his (or her) homework only heaven knows.

Mordecai got wind of what had happened and rent his clothes in mourning. Then Esther found out. She was distraught and sent for her uncle but Mordecai wouldn't come. Esther then dispatched a messenger to Mordecai to find out exactly what had happened (she did her homework). Mordecai sent word back to his foster daughter to go to the king and plead for their people. He knew about the awesome law of the Persians which couldn't be rescinded and she knew about the law which forbade anyone from entering the king's presence unbidden. Unless the king stretched out the golden sceptre to an intruder, death was imminent.

We find protocol today incredible, especially in a culture where the chief officer of the land goes by his nickname. Nor do we know much about the culture of this civilization, but Esther did. Still, she knew she had to do something. She sent word to Mordecai, telling him to assemble all the Jews to be found in Shushan and to fast with her for three days. After that she would go to the king, regardless of the consequences.

## A BANQUET FOR THREE

Esther, a queen in every sense of the word,

donned her royal robes and stood in the forbidden inner court of the king's palace, facing the entrance. When the king caught sight of his beloved queen standing there, he was deeply moved. The queen approached the king and reached out and touched the head of the golden sceptre which he had honorably extended.

Knowing her husband and his peculiarities well, she didn't tell him why she was there. Rather, she invited him to a feast she was going to prepare in his honor with Haman as their guest. The king accepted, and during the banquet he offered his beautiful queen anything she wanted—up to one-half of his kingdom. Her response was simply to ask him to attend another feast on the day following.

Haman was well pleased with himself but seethed with rage at the sight of Mordecai, who deliberately refused to do obeisance to him. Wisely he controlled himself. He could wait another day or two until his moment of revenge would come. When he got home he complained bitterly about the stubborn official to his wife (this practice has its advantages but it can also be dangerous). She, doubtless contaminated by the same feeling of hatred and chagrin, suggested to her husband that he build a gallows seventy-five feet high and ask the king in the morning for Mordecai to be hanged on it. Haman thought this an excellent idea.

Once more he consulted with his wife about this business matter of a mocking employee. This time she reversed herself and warned Ha-

man that Mordecai could be his downfall. How right she was. Where she got her insight is uncertain. Intuition? Reason? Friends? An established reputation of the Jewish people living in exile? The character and potentiality of Mordecai himself? Who knows? At any rate, just prior to this she had suggested, together with friends, that Haman build an impressive gallows where Mordecai would dangle before the eyes of countless onlookers. Now she warns her husband—too late—to think twice before he tries anything with Mordecai. But before they could talk any further, the king's chariot arrived and whisked Haman off for his date with the queen and her husband.

The banquet was perfect. The king was once again deeply moved by his lovely wife and offered her again anything up to one-half of the kingdom. It was now or never. Esther came right to the point as she told her king that a wicked man had plotted against her and her people. When Xerxes demanded to know who this wretched man was, Esther pointed at the dumbfounded Haman. The king rose in rage and retreated into the garden while Haman remained to plead for his life. In his pathetic zeal to exonerate himself, Haman flung himself across the couch on which Esther was reclining just as the king returned to the banquet hall.

The king was furious but listened as one of his favorite attendants whispered into his ear that Haman had built a seventy-five-foot gallows for Mordecai. Ironically, after the first banquet,

Xerxes couldn't sleep. Rather than count sheep, he asked for the records of the past. During this review of events the king discovered that he had never rewarded Mordecai for breaking up a plot against his life. He had therefore just sent orders to publicly praise Mordecai for his alertness, and now Haman (who thought the king was going to honor him) would soon dangle from the same contraption he had hastily built for his mortal enemy.

Xerxes, not given to weighing all matters carefully or in detail, barked out an instant order to hang Haman on his own gallows. And there Haman hung until he died. What a way to go.

## LAWS ARE MADE TO BE BROKEN

Whoever coined this phrase no doubt had some experience with the judicial process. Laws, important as they are, are usually inadequate under certain circumstances. At times they are unjust and ought to be remanded or repudiated. But not so with the laws of the Medes and Persians (to use again another coined phrase). They prided themselves on making a law and standing with it, no matter what! This is a dangerous practice, be it in politics or religion. Man-made laws are often homemade; and though they are designed to do a specific task, there is always the chance that the law created might be inadequate, or even a hoax.

Xerxes had already been trapped by one of his laws when he banished the beautiful Vashti

from his life forever. Would he do it again? Never! With that emotional but logical outburst, the king hung both Haman and his absolute law on the gallows. Letters had already been sent by currier to each province with orders to exterminate every Jew, young and old, women and children, on the thirteenth day of the twelfth month. And it had the seal of the royal signet.

How could Xerxes violate his own law without suffering the dreaded consequences of being branded as an impotent governor? Technically he couldn't. Esther, realizing that the king had already announced the date of execution—and knowing full well the eccentricity and profane pride which rode on his name—again spoke before the king. Falling at his feet, with tears streaming down her glorious cheeks, she pleaded with him to avert this awful tragedy. Xerxes could carry out this dastardly deed; he was quite capable of it. But now he realized that his love for this Jewess, an alien orphan by the name of Hadassah, was far more powerful than hate, and almost as powerful as pride.

Therefore, he found a way around the situation by empowering Mordecai, now sitting in one of the most exalted positions in the land, to issue an edict in the name of the king which would spare the Jewish people. For good measure, Xerxes gave Mordecai his royal signet to seal the proclamation. Esther and her people were spared and the king was not forced to repeat history.

Esther, in a relatively short time, had learned

what so many fail to learn in a lifetime. She had learned how to handle her husband—not how to manipulate him or give in to him, but how to honestly deal with him. She analyzed the situation carefully, taking care lest she crash into his presence with the finesse of a bull in a china shop. Xerxes, at times at least, operated this way. Which was enough reason for Esther not to (can you imagine two bulls in a china shop?).

We hear a lot about the so-called incompatibility of couples. And, we must hasten to add, too much of it is pure nonsense, actually. It would be rare, extremely rare, for two people (especially a man and a woman) to be completely incompatible. There are just too many things going for a man and a woman to be incompatible. Two men, or two women, maybe; but not two members of the opposite sex. They might be selfish, proud, thoughtless, arrogant, rude, stubborn, mean, and immature—but incompatible? Men and women fight each other, do all sort of evil against themselves, and continually vie with each other for supremacy, yes; but they also form an alliance between each other such as two men or two women have never known—nor will they ever know. Why? Because men and women were created for each other. Attitudes and situations may cause incompatibility, but a man and a woman are far from incompatible.

However, under the circumstances, certain situations made Esther and Xerxes about as incompatible as two people could be. But they made

it. Was it because Esther was such a beautiful woman, a shrewd manipulator, or because she shed some awfully persuasive tears? Hardly. This helped (so did the memory of what Xerxes did to Vashti). Esther won because she had to win! To save her marriage, she broke a law which just wasn't broken in ancient Persia—but her marriage was more important than anything else. That's why she kept her marriage intact. Her inner beauty excelled her outward attractiveness.

## THE OTHER SIDE OF THE COIN

King Xerxes has gone down in history as a successful, handsome, proud, and sometimes violent monarch—and not a little eccentric. His pagan Persian ways were a far cry from the restricted monotheism of Esther which she had held in reserve as she traveled incognito for so long. Apart from the Bible, Esther, historically, is an unknown. But we know her, thanks to some fine Hebrew writer-historian, as a beautiful, gracious, magnanimous, deeply pious, virtuous and patriotic queen. Rarely, outwardly speaking, have two people been so potentially incompatible.

Esther, in spite of her charm and ability to persuade the king, would have been powerless to do anything about her desperate situation if Xerxes hadn't wanted to go along with it. She had no power, no army standing behind her, no devilish guile, no capacity to blackmail, and no special access to a divine power. Remember, she

had submerged her Jewish identity for so long that she probably had gotten a little out of touch (or at least out of practice) with her God. Of course, this is only speculation; she may, indeed, have been driven much closer to her God, the God of her fathers, during this ordeal. And she may have been a quiet believer all along. Even so, there is no indication that she could extend her own scepter and call a legion or two of angels to fight her battle. She, like most of us, was on her own—and she did very well. Even so, the point is clear: if Xerxes hadn't wanted to spare her life along with her people, he wouldn't have had to make the concession he did, running the risk of reneging on his word— which could have been interpreted as a sign of weakness by his not too friendly enemies. He had a lot to gain by honoring Esther, but he had a lot to lose as well. The important thing is that he chose to honor her passionate pleading.

Although Esther deserves much credit for her heroic efforts to save a marriage, it would have all gone for nought if Xerxes hadn't gone along with it. It takes two to tangle, this we know; but it only takes one to actually doom a marriage.

Xerxes as well as Esther wanted their marriage to endure and that's why it did. No matter how right one party may be, or how persuasive, or even how manipulative, if a marriage is to endure and thrive, both parties must want it to be successful.

Esther and Xerxes do remind us that "where there's a will, there's a way"; but they are saying

something considerably more important: *where there is no will, there is no way.* Strange, isn't it, how half a will in a marriage cannot overcome the other half. But that's how marriages fall apart. Incompatibility has too often become a facade behind which a stubborn marriage hides. It isn't true that incompatibility is the culprit in most cases of so-called incompatibility. It is the refusal of one or the other (or both) to work at saving a marriage like Esther and Xerxes did. And it may be even more strange to realize that this thing called incompatibility has often strengthened a union of two people from vastly different cultures and backgrounds and temperaments and dispositions.

Could it be that incompatibility is actually a myth and that the real enemy is pride and stubbornness and lust and immaturity and thoughtlessness and just plain cruelty? Maybe Esther and Xerxes could answer that. On second thought, maybe they have.

1. Discuss the similarities and dissimilarities between the marriages of Xerxes-Esther and David-Bathsheba.
2. People often do things they regret later on. Xerxes was no exception. What is the difference between breaking an oath and keeping one when the net result is incompatible with the original oath? How hard should we try to get around so-called irreversible situations?
3. Had Esther abandoned her faith in God while living incognito? Is the Book of Esther basically a book on racial prejudice? If not, what are some of the other important theses?
4. Why would Esther and Xerxes be such likely candidates for incompatibility? Is it true that marital incompatibility is probably more fiction than truth?

Explain: *The Myth of Incompatibility.* Is incompatibility used more as an excuse than as a valid reason for breaking up a marriage?

5. How could Esther be the wife of a pagan king and still maintain her godliness? Can a person be a silent believer? for how long? How should a person like Esther live with a man like Xerxes?

6. Are some laws made to be broken? which ones? when? Did God break any of His laws by blessing His people via a woman who was living incognito?

7. Is it true that one spouse can wreck a marriage if he or she wants to, regardless how the other partner tries to make it work? Is this the same as incompatibility?

FOR FURTHER READING . . .

The Book of Esther

A CASE STUDY . . .

Tom and Judy are having trouble reconciling their marriage. Judy, hurt by one marriage failure already, argues that she and Tom are incompatible. She is sorry for her indiscretions and Tom, although he finds it hard to forgive, is willing to try, with God's help. Judy still maintains that their children do not get along too well with each other, and that she and Tom have less in common than she thought they had when they married. YOU ARE STILL HOPING TO SAVE A CRUMBLING SECOND MARRIAGE RATHER THAN RUN THE RISK OF ANOTHER DIVORCE AND ITS SUBSEQUENT COMPLICATIONS. HOW WOULD YOU GO ABOUT TRYING TO SHOW HER THE FAULTINESS OF HER REASONING (IN THE LIGHT OF THE CHAPTER)?

# II

# PONTIUS AND PROCULA

## Dreams and Nightmares

*Leave that good man alone; for I had a terrible nightmare concerning him. . . .*

Matthew 27:19

More has been written about the feminine mystique than has been understood. I suppose that's why it's still a mystique.

We know about as much about feminine hunches as we do about Pontius Pilate's wife.

She had a hunch and it turned out to be right. A woman's intuition is often uncanny. Pilate got the message; Procula* saw to that. The real problem might not be the intuitive nature of women (and wives) as much as it is dealing with these intuitions.

### THE FEMININE HUNCH

Volumes could be filled with stranger-than-fiction stories about feminine hunches. Yes, men dream dreams and have visions, and not a few of

---

* I am indebted to Paul Maier's book, *Pontius Pilate* for the name of Pilate's wife.

them have pretty good hunches too. But men are not noted for an uncanny intuition, not in the sense we're talking about. This is one of those mysterious dimensions which separate the sexes. And why not? For ages men and women have bemoaned the fact that they can't understand each other. Which is true. But what a shame it would be for a man and a woman if there was not even a shred of mystery left in their marriage.

Indelibly etched on my mind is an experience I had before I was a husband and a father. I stopped with a friend at his home for a few moments and met a hysterical young mother head on. She was in her house with their two small boys when all of a sudden she had a strange premonition that something was wrong. There was no warning of any kind—just an over-powering feeling. She fled from the living room (or was it kitchen?) into the boys' bedroom, where she found that the youngest had already turned a deathly blue.

The older brother had somehow emptied the piggy bank and was placing the pennies, one at a time, into his little brother's mouth. The lovely young mother was horrified, but did what her feminine nature dictated. She grabbed the little fellow by his feet, held him upside down, and shook him vigorously, scattering pennies in every direction. She then flipped him over and pounded fresh air into his lungs. They both survived. When she saw her husband, her composure collapsed and hysteria took over.

The question is clear, isn't it? Who or what told her something was wrong? Unless we are complete skeptics (or hopeless pragmatists), it seems a bit foolish not to allow for the feminine hunch. We can also go to the other extreme and lean too heavily on feminine intuition. Incredible mistakes have been made because we have leaned too far one way or the other.

Procula suffered a painful dream—possibly even a nightmare. Whatever the case, it was traumatic enough for her to risk her wifely propriety as she interfered in the affairs of her husband.

Although men do have hunches (check the stock market or the race track if in doubt), they operate more or less in spite of them. Could it be that there is a divine purpose behind the feminine nature which gives balance to the union of two members of the opposite sex? We talk about the emotional woman and the logical male (which also can be a dangerous oversimplification), but we have also seen the hyperemotional male properly subdued by a logically cool female. Even so, this is all the more reason why men and women need each other: not to compete necessarily (a certain amount is natural and desirable), but to complement.

During a state-wide family conference I had the privilege of sharing speaking responsibilities with a guest minister from another denomination. I was also handling the platform duties (you know, making the commercials). As the conference progressed, a certain amount of

friendly bantering developed between the guest speaker and myself. Finally, after another one of my off-beat commentaries, my wife slipped me a nonverbal but highly communicative message which said, LEAVE THAT MAN ALONE! I did. Enough was enough. The conference ended on a particularly high note, spiritually and otherwise. Even though the audience was enjoying the friendly bantering, my spouse felt intuitively that I had pushed the levity far enough. Her hunch was right; and her propriety (meddling in my affairs) was proper (even though I resented it just a bit at the time).

Perhaps all of us could pray a prayer something like this—daily, or maybe even hourly on some days: *Lord, make me sensitive to the whims, feelings, and hunches of my partner today, even if it hurts.*

## THE FEMININE PUNCH

Personally, I think Procula did what she did, not because she was a meddlesome wife, but because her dream was so real—so terrifying—she had to act. Maybe she was a nagging wife who hung around in the shadows waiting for her husband to make a mistake, but I doubt it.

This poses an eternal question. Whom was she trying to protect? Her husband? Blessed is the wife who tries to keep her man from falling flat on his face. Even more blessed is the woman who can do this unobtrusively.

Was she trying to protect Jesus? She knew

that her husband had deep within him a sense of justice. She knew that he knew Jesus was innocent of the absurd charges brought against Him. Did she cringe when she saw a just man hang on the verge of death? Did it bother her to see the innocent victimized?

Or was she trying to protect herself? Did she have a dreadful fear of what would happen to her if Pontius Pilate couldn't handle this scene? Jerusalem had been a troublesome assignment for her husband, but it was a pretty fair position. If Pilate blew this one, they could be banished into a miserable new assignment in the middle of nowhere. Her pomp and circumstance could vanish over night. Is this what she dreaded?

The fact is, she could have been troubled over all three: her husband, herself, and the stranger from Galilee. Undoubtedly she knew something about Jesus. Rumors traveled quickly then as they do now, and they reached the governor as well as the man on the street. Pilate knew that Jesus was not guilty of the charges; he also knew that Jesus posed a threat to his regime. Therefore, after weighing the pros and cons—the future of Jesus as well as his own—he decided to scourge Jesus publicly, and let Him go. That should have satisfied the mob but it didn't. They wanted Jesus executed, then and there.

Procula, badly shaken by her traumatic dream, was watching in the shadows. She felt the agony of her husband's dilemma. She knew what was going through his mind—the ugly crowd with its impassioned curses—the no-non-

sense hierarchy in Rome—the previous trouble with these stubborn people in this mad city. When she realized that Pontius Pilate, the governor but also her husband, was wavering, she hastily scribbled a note and sent it to her husband: LEAVE THAT GOOD MAN ALONE, FOR I HAD A TERRIBLE NIGHTMARE CONCERNING HIM. . . . This was undoubtedly a bold thing for a woman to do in the first century, and very improper—but she did it anyway.

Here is where we must admire Procula. She could have kept silent and then greeted her husband when he came home with those awful words, "I told you so." Rather, she chose to hit him with a potent weapon, the *feminine punch.*

## ON REMEMBERING PROCULA

Let's examine what happened more closely. Procula told Pontius what she thought without beating around the bush. Her message was brief and to the point. There are times—and may God grant us the wisdom to know when—when we ought to skirt the issue; and there are times when we must come right to the heart of the matter. How many marriages have ebbed away because of a wishy-washy approach to trouble spots we'll never know. But there are many. Why she didn't run up and whisper in his ear instead of writing a note is not ours to question, perhaps. But it might suggest that if we don't have the nerve (or opportunity) to come right out with it, there are alternatives.

One night after I had retired somewhat later

than my wife, I found a page torn from a popular magazine lying on my pillow. I crawled under the covers and began to read, wondering what message she was trying to get across. The message was unquestionably although not painfully clear. It was a tribute to the virtue of being on time. I personally happen to dislike tardiness but I abhor being too early (such a waste of time). Consequently I evidently cut it too close at times, which of course results in the vice called tardiness. I happened to turn the page over when I finished reading and what did I discover. Another story dealing with one of my own pet peeves regarding my little sweetheart who was sleeping so innocently beside me. Resisting the temptation to awaken her, I made a little arrangement of the torn page which she couldn't possibly miss in the morning, turned off the light, and vanished into pleasant dreams. We were both successful; we had communicated effectively without saying a word.

Not only did Procula come right to the point in her own way, she timed it well. This was the golden moment. A few minutes later would have been eternally too late. Watching him agonize with this awful decision demanded action. Dispatching a messenger to the governor would give him a little extra time to wrestle with his decision. Pilate has been pegged as both a ruthless, selfish man and a coward. Maybe he was. But cowards and ruthless people normally act first and think later. Pilate was doing it the other way

around. Procula not only gave him an excuse to deliberate a moment longer, she also gave him an excuse to follow her hunch. Then he could come home and say, "I told *you* so." In a very real sense, she was putting herself out on a limb for the man she loved. The note was terse, almost abrupt in its command. She didn't say, "If you love me, you'll let this man go," but it was implied. Procula's act wasn't a test of his love—it was proof of her love. There is quite a difference!

There is one more dimension of this scene worth noting. Procula not only told her husband what to do, she told him why. Without a lengthy discussion, she simply said that she had a dream—a bad one. Therefore, knowing that she had no chance of convincing him with a simple wifely memo, she added the reason why she was doing it. Since she had this incredible dream—which was doubtless some kind of omen—she knew she had to inform the governor. She couldn't do otherwise.

This is beautiful. So often we lower the boom on our spouse without a shred of a hint why. If there's a good reason for suggesting something, we ought to come out with it. If not, the suggestion is probably worthless, or close to it.

## ON DOING WHAT IS RIGHT

We will never know if Procula was trying to save her husband from untold misery, rescue

Jesus from madmen, or salve her own conscience. But it doesn't matter. Tradition tells us that Pilate, like Lady Macbeth, couldn't wash the blood from his hands and finally took his own life. This we don't know for certain, but we do know that Pontius Pilate's wife never went down in history as an infamous Lady Pilate. Why? Not because she tried to please her husband but because she tried to do what was right.

A marriage counselor once told a young husband who was going crazy trying to please his wife to quit trying to please her. "The harder you try," he said, "the worse it'll get." He told the young husband to start doing what was right and then he'd please her. It worked. It still does (most of the time). When she sulked, he spanked (wow!). When she was lonely, he called her from the office. Once in awhile he brought flowers home—for no reason at all (except that wives like both flowers and surprises). Pretty soon she started fixing things he liked (instead of what she liked) for dinner (but not all the time) and vacuumed the house after the TV game instead of during it. Before long they discovered that by doing right they were actually pleasing each other. An unsalvageable marriage was salvaged.

Procula did what she felt was right. Pilate didn't. They both kept on dreaming as they laid their weary heads to rest each night; but it was Pontius, not Procula, who had the nightmares.

It is extremely difficult to do what is right and to do it inoffensively. It is difficult to scold

140

without screaming—to tell the truth even when we know it will hurt—to remind without nagging—to wait for an opportune moment. But marriages demand this on occasion. Some marriages demand it quite often.

A very well-known clergyman, gifted, perceptive, and unquestionably a righteous man, was once praised by his son who stated he could never remember his father saying a harsh word to his mother. This is quite a tribute (unless the wife and mother happens to be an angel or a hopeless, unreasonable creature—then it would not pay to say much at all, would it?).

Even so, I would venture to hazard a guess that there were moments in their marriage when silently, with no fanfare, this model husband and wife put a few well-chosen words together in order to set the record straight. In fact, I know they did; but it wasn't done at the dinner table (where many parents come unglued) or in the family car on the way to church on Sunday morning.

Procula, quietly and discreetly, communicated with her husband that he was about to do something he might regret. It is this wise discretion, not the avoidance of unpleasantries, that keeps dreams from becoming nightmares.

Mark Twain and Harry Truman combined to suggest a thought for the ending of this treatise on dreams and nightmares. The former president of the United States is reported to have kept this saying on his desk in the White House:

141

# ALWAYS DO RIGHT. THIS WILL GRATIFY SOME PEOPLE AND ASTONISH THE REST.

Mark Twain
To the Young People's Society
Greenpoint Presbyterian Church
Brooklyn
(February 16, 1901)[1]

1. What is meant by the term *feminine mystique?* Is there such a thing as a *masculine mystique?* If so, what might it be?
2. How much faith should be put in a hunch (or intuition)? Is this going contrary to a devout faith in God? Does God speak through intuition? What about the understanding and interpretation of dreams?
3. Is the following prayer valid? "Lord, make me sensitive to the whims, feelings, and hunches of my partner today, even if it hurts." Why? Why not?
4. When should a wife try to protect (or guide) her husband? When should a husband try to protect (or guide) his wife? What is the difference between *meddling* and *assisting?* What is the difference between *nagging* and *pleading?*
5. How important is timing in communication? Give some examples.
6. Are some people considerably more difficult to live with than others? What are some of the traits you consider very difficult to live with? Is "peace at any price" a vice or a virtue in marriage?
7. Many couples are guilty of chiding, nagging, or berating each other publicly. Why do they do this? What can be done about it?

FOR FURTHER READING . . .

Luke 3, 23; Matthew 27; Mark 15; John 18, 19; Acts 3, 4, 13; I Timothy 6; I Corinthians 13:4-7

---

[1] John Bartlett, *Familiar Quotations*, 13th edition (Boston: Little, Brown and Co.), p. 679.

A CASE STUDY . . .

Tom and Judy finally reconciled their marital problems and worked out a satisfactory solution. Their next to the oldest daughter wants to get married, but both Tom and Judy dislike the timing even though they do approve of her choice very much. Judy, alas, had a dream in which she was dramatically warned not to allow her daughter to get married to this man. She didn't say anything at first to anyone, but it weighed heavily on her and finally she went to her clergyman for advice. YOU ARE THE CLERGYMAN. WHAT WOULD YOU ADVISE? WOULD YOU INVOLVE THE WHOLE FAMILY? HOW?

# 12

# ANANIAS AND SAPPHIRA

## Compatibility at Its Worst

*A man named Ananias with his wife Sapphira sold a piece of property . . . but kept part of the money for himself. . . .*

Acts 5:1, 2

Not all husbands and wives are partners in business. Many husbands do the bookkeeping, make the investments, but leave final instructions locked up thoughtfully in a safe deposit box with the key safely tucked away in *her* jewelry chest.

On the other hand, many wives balance the checkbook, pay the bills, compute taxes, and pester their broker with shrewd insights into the drift of the stock market without the aid but with the blessings of their husbands.

Ananias and Sapphira did their business (and monkey business) together.

### ON BEING COMPATIBLE

Here is a couple who were compatible. Too much so. Let's see what actually happened.

The early Christian church at this time was a struggling band of renegades (in the eyes of the orthodox Hebrew community). Their numbers were small. Their faith was at best spotty: some believed with an incredible trust; others were running scared.

To align yourself with the early Christians in Jerusalem was something like joining a radical enclave in Berkeley. The early Christians were tolerated by the majority, perhaps, but despised and feared by the Jewish leaders. Consequently, to become a Christian often meant disgrace. Men lost their positions. Families disowned—even disinherited—heretical members who aligned themselves with this growing "sect."

This forced the early Christian community into a communal life style. They pooled their resources, subsidized the poor widows, gave sustenance to believers who were forced out of their jobs. No one went hungry. In short, it was a happy but somewhat fearful group of believers who loved one another so much that it showed.

## BARNABAS, THE PACESETTER

One day a native from the island of Cyprus, a convert, sold a piece of property. He took the money and gave it to Peter, the natural leader of the struggling commune. Peter was doubtless grateful for this generosity and presumably made much of the situation. Everyone was impressed and deeply moved. Barnabas, because of his genuine generosity, was made hero for the day—and rightfully so. The early church was

teetering on the brink of extinction: it could have gone either way. Barnabas came through and gave the early church a much-needed encouragement, not only in resources but by example.

In the same congregation there were two other members who watched the whole proceedings with interest. They saw the gratitude swell in the hearts of their fellow believers. They watched Barnabas become the center of attraction and their emotions were scrambled to bits. As fellow believers they were most grateful to Barnabas. As affection starved members they felt that with a little effort they could get a chunk of this loving attention for themselves. What they did is common knowledge. Why they did it may be less obvious. The tragic result—well, that's another story.

## IT TAKES TWO TO TANGLE

The world is full of clever songs and biting indictments and comical remarks about the rivalry between man and woman.

Shortly before I was married the boys had a surprise stag party in my honor. As I walked innocently up to the Bob Lundberg residence (they were the decoys), the door swung open and I was met with a solid blast of Lerner and Loewe. Henry Higgins was enlightening Colonel Pickering in *My Fair Lady*, reminding him that when you let a woman in your life your serenity is through. Somehow, Higgins instinctively

seemed to feel that a woman's primary goal is to completely overhaul a man (or at least remodel him considerably). For some women, this is their major objective, and they go at it in varying degrees: some nibble away at their man while others go after him with a sledge. But their ultimate goal is the same.

Before too long, Eliza Doolittle seized equal time and lambasted Henry Higgins with a solid left to his reasonably well-protected bachelorhood, crying, "Just you wait, Henry Higgins!" The rest of the story you know quite well.

The battle between the sexes has not diminished considerably during the last few generations. In fact, the tempo may be quickening. There could be some interesting days ahead not excluding alimony-paying wives and court domesticated husbands.

In-fighting between man and woman—not excepting those married to each other—is nothing new. Evidently, Ananias and Sapphira had settled their petty little differences as well as their fundamental grievances prior to their private examination of Barnabas, the hero from Cyprus, as they concentrated on their conniving camaraderie. Let's eavesdrop on their discussion.

A penny for your thoughts, Ananias!

HUH? GUESS I WAS DAYDREAMING. SORRY. A PENNY FOR MY THOUGHTS? THEY'RE NOT WORTH A PENNY, DEAR.

Come on, now. Don't be so modest. I know

something is bothering you. Maybe it's the same thing that's been troubling me.

DO YOU THINK SO? NO, YOU'LL NEVER GUESS. IT'S NOTHING, REALLY. JUST ANOTHER ONE OF MY MOODS. IT'LL PASS OVER—IT ALWAYS DOES.

Listen, honey. We've been married too long to try to hide anything. Come on, confess. It can't be that bad.

THIS TIME I'M AFRAID IT IS. I'M NOT VERY PROUD OF WHAT I'M THINKING.

Let me guess what it is? May I?

SURE, IF IT'LL MAKE YOU FEEL ANY BETTER.

You're thinking about what Barnabas did. Right?

HOW'D YOU KNOW?

It's written all over your face.

DOES IT SHOW THAT MUCH?

It sure does. But don't worry about it. I'm the only one who can read your mind.

SAPPHIRA, SOMETIMES YOU AMAZE ME. WHAT DO YOU THINK WE OUGHT TO DO?

What do you mean?

WE'VE GOT SOME PROPERTY WE COULD SELL. THE GOOD LORD KNOWS WE NEED EVERYTHING WE CAN GET. YESTERDAY THERE WERE THIRTY-EIGHT MORE PEOPLE FOR SUPPER. EVERY DAY IT'S THE SAME STORY. NOW WE'VE GOT LAWYERS, PHYSICIANS, TENT MAKERS—ALL OF THEM HAVE LOST THEIR JOBS. THREE MORE WIDOWS YESTERDAY, TOO.

I know. We can't let those little ones go hungry either. There's a couple of people in there I don't trust, though. I think they're more interested in the food than their souls, really.

I THINK YOU'RE BEING A LITTLE HARSH, MY DEAR. IT'S TOO SOON TO JUDGE THEM. LET'S GIVE THEM A LITTLE MORE TIME BEFORE WE LOWER THE BOOM. OKAY?

I suppose you're right. What do you think we should do?

I THINK WE OUGHT TO TAKE OUR CHANCES AND SELL OUR PROPERTY RIGHT NOW. YOU SAW WHAT HAPPENED WHEN BARNABAS SOLD HIS PROPERTY. THAT'S THE LEAST WE CAN DO.

And the most, Mr. Ananias! That's all we have, you know.

I KNOW. DON'T REMIND ME. BUT WHAT CHOICE DO WE HAVE? AS LONG AS I'M A BELIEVER I CAN'T WORK IN JERUSALEM. WE MAY HAVE TO LEAVE ANYWAY, SOONER OR LATER.

Listen, honey, I've got an idea. Let's sell the property. Then we'll take some of the money and put it aside and pretend that we only got so much for it. No one'll ever know the difference, we'll still get all the credit—you know, like Barnabas did. And if things don't work out, well—we'll have something to fall back on.

NOW WAIT JUST A MINUTE. ARE YOU SUGGESTING THAT WE. . . .

Oh, come on, dear. I'm not suggesting anything of the kind. It just makes good sense. We'll actually give a sizable amount to Peter, but in an emergency we won't be broke. It just makes good sense, Ananias. We're not hurting anybody. After all, we don't even have to sell the property in the first place.

SAPPHIRA, YOU MIGHT HAVE SOMETHING THERE. I WAS IMPRESSED WITH WHAT BARNABAS DID. REALLY I WAS. BUT I COULDN'T QUITE SEE MYSELF BEING THAT GENEROUS.

Let's do it, Ananias. As you said, the Lord knows we need every penny we can get. . . .

## A COMFORTABLE COMPATIBILITY

And so Ananias and Sapphira concocted their seemingly harmless little scheme. Or was it? Maybe all they wanted was a little more attention. Some people do starve for a bit of recognition. It could be that Ananias and Sapphira, believers that they were (nonbelievers would hardly run the risk at this stage of the game to pose as believers—would they?), were not yet sure of the outcome of this new faith. After all, Christ had proved Himself a worthy leader, and many were thoroughly convinced that He was the long awaited Messiah; but they were not so sure then how Peter and Christianity would endure. Therefore, it would be rather natural for them to put aside a bit for a rainy day.

If God was punishing them simply for what they did, we would find it difficult to understand, much less justify. But if God was afraid that their kind of hypocrisy might become the rule rather than the exception, the situation leans in a totally different direction.

We now know that the existence of this primitive congregation was soon to be severely threatened. Very shortly, enormous pressure—from both within as well as without—was exerted on the church. Its very survival was in jeopardy. God knew this. Somehow, Peter must have sensed it.

Consequently, God dramatized in a traumatic way the dire consequence of hypocrisy within the fellowship. By removing Ananias and

Sapphira from the scene, He was not necessarily punishing them for a tragic error in judgment as much as He was indicting hypocrisy and warning, not only the early Christian church, but the church at large ever since. God just doesn't go around striking people dead for grandstanding, but He is death on hypocrisy; for He knows that like cancer it can gnaw at the heart of a congregation until it is destroyed. That God could have preserved His church in another way is quite possible; but He chose this way, not because He was ruthless but because He knew what lay ahead. God knew that internal dissent, tawdry politicking, and subtle hypocrisy would slam the doors shut in a hurry. Hypocrisy is far more damaging than persecution.

## BRINGING OUT THE BEST

Ananias might have been more guilty than Sapphira. We don't know. Whatever transpired as far as the motives were concerned we may never know. What we do know is this: they both agreed—together—to do what they did. They analyzed the whole situation until their clever little scheme evolved. Deep down I cannot help but feel they knew it was wrong, but I also feel that they never dreamt of its far reaching implications. Most of us seldom see all of the inevitable consequences of our deeds.

Somewhere, somehow, if either Ananias or Sapphira would have put their foot down and said, "No, I cannot go along with this," the

whole chapter would have been a different one. One of the greatest tragedies in marriage is that it seems to be far easier to bring out the worst rather than the best in each other.

Unfortunately, Ananias and Sapphira, in a moment of weakness, brought out the worst in each other—a malady which too easily becomes habit forming.

*Blessed is the man who brings the best out of his woman, and the woman who brings the best out of her man.*

1. It has been suggested that no two people are completely incompatible. What does it mean that a couple can be too compatible?
2. Can a couple be starved for affection and attention just as an individual can? Does this occur very often? What happens? What can be done about it?
3. Men and women are good for each other for many reasons. List as many reasons as you can think of. What are some of the reasons (or potential reasons) why a man and a woman are not good for each other?
4. How accurate is the reading of one partner by another? Can a husband or a wife completely hide his or her true feelings (e.g., hurt, pride, disgust, suspicion, gratitude, fear, hate, love, disappointment, etc.)?
5. Is it a valid assumption to expect that a good marriage has a built-in check and balance system? What does this mean? How does it operate?
6. God doesn't go around striking people dead for grandstanding or cheating. Why did God strike this couple dead? Wasn't there a better way, or at least another way? Do you agree with this thesis?
7. How can we bring the best rather than the worst out of our spouse? Is it possible for this to become habit forming?

FOR FURTHER READING . . .

Acts 1—5; Ephesians 5:22-33; I Corinthians 4; James 1; I Corinthians 10:13

A CASE STUDY . . .

Judy and Tom were extremely disappointed in their
minister and his counseling. He told them to forget the
dream and to concentrate on their Christian life. They
took offense because they expected more charity or at
least some understanding. This became a real sore spot in
their home life; and soon they began to criticize him
openly, knocked the church, found fault with his family,
and became convinced that they ought to do something
about it. Over a few cups of coffee with several church
friends, they began to plan how to oust their minister.
YOU ARE A CLOSE FRIEND AND HAVE BEEN IN-
VITED TO COFFEE WHERE YOU WERE INSTRUCT-
ED HOW YOU COULD PLAY A ROLE IN THIS.
HOW WOULD YOU REACT? WHAT WOULD YOU
DO? WHAT SHOULD YOU DO?

# 13

# PRISCILLA AND AQUILA

## The Liberated Wife

*Apollos began to speak boldly in the synagogue;
but when Priscilla and Aquila heard him, they
took him and expounded to him the way of God
more accurately.*

Acts 18:26

In Scripture, the man is usually mentioned
first (*Adam* and *Eve*, *Abraham* and *Sarah*, *Samson* and *Delilah*, *Ananias* and *Sapphira*). A notable exception occurs with this couple, Priscilla
and Aquila. Out of the *six* times they are mentioned, Priscilla is mentioned first *four* times. Is
this an accident? Is it inconsequential? Or is
there some hidden significance?

Let's try to find out.

### WHAT'S IN A NAME?

When my wife and I chose a name for our
daughter, we were quite aware that *Laurie* was a
derivative of *Laura*. When we added *Lee* as her

middle name we came pretty close to *Lorelei*, who, in German folklore, was a siren of the Rhine who lured fishermen to destruction by the spell of her song. What a handle to hang on an unsuspecting babe!

I suppose this points up a characteristic of our culture: we don't take the literal meaning of a given name too seriously. Rather, we prefer the sound (and certain spellings) to the sentiment, as we both agreed that *Laurie Lee* sounded pretty good and looked pretty nice. And *Laura* (or *Laurie*) was a long way from *Lorelei* in meaning, which should put those fishermen at ease if our daughter should ever settle down near the Rhine.

In analyzing the names *Priscilla* and *Aquila* we discover that *Priscilla* seems to come from the Latin *Prisca*, meaning "old woman." Therefore, *Priscilla* literally means "little old woman." *Aquila* seems to fare a bit better. His name means "eagle." Now, if this isn't an unlikely combination: a "little old woman" married to an "eagle." From all evidence at hand, *Aquila* might have been more a "little old man" and *Priscilla* a "soaring eagle."

Amazingly enough, in every Scriptural instance, Priscilla and Aquila are mentioned together. This togetherness might have a certain significance as well. Let's explore this a little further.

## WHO IS PRISCILLA?

According to Dr. Luke and his good friend

Paul, Priscilla was a tentmaker along with her husband. She was also a homemaker and a skilled lay student of Christian doctrine. Any more than this we must read into the sketchy accounts given in the six brief mentions by the two inspired writers (Acts 18:2, 18, 26; Rom. 16:3; I Cor. 16:19; II Tim. 4:19).

Here is where the fun begins. Ruth Hoppin, a housewife with a B.A. degree in chemistry, penned a book which she published herself after fifteen rejections by religious publishers. *Priscilla, Author of Epistle to the Hebrews*, was released in 1969 after years of research and writing. About a year later her book picked up momentum and people began to take notice.

Although we will not argue here for or against the Priscillan authorship of the Book of Hebrews, Mrs. Hoppin's concern is worthy of consideration. She claimed that Hebrews is the product of a female mind. Maybe so. She was also not a little concerned because she felt that women have been wronged in other parts of the Bible too. This she illustrated by arguing that Eve at least agreed with the serpent but Adam succumbed without a murmur of protest.[1] This is a more interesting than convincing argument for women's liberation, however.

The Bible does seem to be dominated by male authors, but this alone is hardly discriminatory. However, Ruth Hoppin has put her finger on

---

[1] From an interview with Ruth Hoppin in the S.F. *Sunday Examiner and Chronicle*, Feb. 14, 1971, p. 6.

something. Priscilla probably was much more than a tentmaker-housewife, just as Paul was much more than a tentmaker-preacher. In my judgment, Priscilla was probably quite capable of authoring the Epistle to the Hebrews. Going one step further, I would also suggest that she probably towered over her husband in ability and intellect—and maybe spirit. However, Priscilla was a liberated woman. Somehow, she had been set free.

## WHAT SET PRISCILLA FREE?

Let me suggest three thoughts that might give an insight into Priscilla's liberation. The first is this: she didn't seem to be mad at anyone. She had no axe to grind. She kept her place while she put woman on the map.

Priscilla and Aquila rolled with the punches. Maybe they enjoyed traveling, but few enjoy moving, moving, moving. Yet Priscilla and Aquila did just that: from Rome (thanks to the unfriendly Claudius) to Corinth (two years) to Ephesus (three years) to Rome again (five to ten years), and back to Ephesus. All of these latter moves were to better the work of the Lord, not because there were better tentmaking prospects elsewhere. Their motives were not indulgent.

Priscilla opened her home and took Paul in. Then Priscilla and Aquila told Paul to lay down his needle. They could earn enough to support all three, which freed Paul to argue, persuade, preach, and rap with the skeptics in the market-

place and with the Jews in the synagogue. When he came home, tired but joyous in his work, Priscilla had the soup on. After soup, Paul and Priscilla (or should it be Priscilla and Paul?) no doubt hammered away at the strategy of the gospel while Aquila took it all in as he sharpened the needles for another day of tentmaking. This went on in several cities on more than one continent.

Priscilla was free because she didn't have to compete with either Paul or Aquila. She accepted them for what they were and they did the same. No one was uptight (or jealous or agitating or climbing or shoving or resentful). Priscilla and Aquila happily discovered their role in life—and Priscilla just happened to be more heavily endowed than her husband. This should hardly surprise us; it happens every day.

## POOR APOLLOS

Priscilla also found liberation, not in elevating herself to the stature of the brilliant, eloquent Apollos, a native of Alexandria, but in bringing Apollos up to her level.

Apollos was extremely well learned in Scripture (Old Testament—the New Testament wasn't compiled yet) and knew the Jewish religion inside out. Then he was converted to Christianity and began to preach. And what a preacher he was! The trouble with his preaching wasn't the style but the content. He merely had half a gospel. He was preaching only after the baptism

of John and had missed the rest of the good news.

Priscilla undoubtedly could have clobbered him, maybe even destroyed him. So what did she do? She and Aquila invited the brilliant, dedicated Apollos into their home and wrapped their arms of love around the young convert, bringing him the rest of the way into the grandeur of Christian truth.

They did so well with their young protégé that people flocked to hear him. A kind of hero worship arose as his audience began to compare him with the incomparable Paul, causing an unfortunate cleavage among the believers. Priscilla, bless her heart, found true liberation as she took an inferior person and not only brought him up to her level, but gave him enough momentum to soar even beyond her. Now who is the eagle?

Even to this day there are those who believe that Apollos is the one who penned the ingenious letter to the Hebrew Christians. Who knows? The Epistle to the Hebrews might well have been the result of two great minds, Priscilla and Apollos, as they pored over the history and theology of the Old Testament, brilliantly showing the hand of God throughout the Old as it was fulfilled in the New.

## LEAVE A LITTLE DUST

Priscilla, brilliant scholar that she presumably was, was also a beautiful homemaker. Paul felt comfortable in their home. So did Apollos. But

even more important, Aquila felt at home in his own home. Beautiful!

Rachel Conrad Wahlberg has penned a book with an intriguing title: *Leave a Little Dust.*[2] To help a woman adjust to her many roles (wife, mother, homemaker, careerist, neighbor, citizen), the author suggests that she should feel free not to be perfect. "I believe men would rather have you prepare a simple meal and be happy about it than go to hours of trouble and be grim when you get it on the table," writes Mrs. Wahlberg.

Evidently Priscilla learned one of the lessons the truly liberated woman has learned: creativity can become a part of everyday life. Priscilla combined her tentmaking skills with hospitality and marital compatibility and theological studies and possibly writing. And even more, she did it all while on the move. No wonder Aquila and Priscilla are always mentioned together. Priscilla was a liberated woman, but in her liberation she set her husband (and other men) free.

*We are only truly liberated when we are able and willing to set others free.*

1. The women's liberation movement has many facets to it. What are some of the underlying reasons why it has become such an issue?
2. How can a woman set a man free? How can a man set a woman free? Should they?
3. The Bible has often been charged with revealing an

---

[2] Fortress Press, Philadelphia, 1971.

antiwoman bias. Do you think this is true? How many names of women can you mention that are given prominence in Scripture? Is this true also of other similar religious literature?
4. Priscilla, according to this chapter, has seemingly made a name for herself. Do I have the right to do this with the limited amount of information available? What data might validate my thesis? contradict it?
5. How would you describe the truly liberated wife? the truly liberated husband? the truly liberated couple?
6. Historically, what has Christianity done for marriage? for individuals?
7. Do you agree with the final statement: "We are only truly liberated when we are able and willing to set others free"? Why or why not?


FOR FURTHER READING . . .

Acts 18; Romans 16; I Corinthians 16; II Timothy 4; Ephesians 5:22; Genesis 2:18; 3:16

A CASE STUDY . . .

Tom and Judy's new dilemma now is this: Tom's youngest brother, who is somewhat of a genius, has dropped out of the university because of his hang-ups. He has ability written all over him but is down on most everything and everybody. Judy believes in him and has high hopes for his future. She wants him to come and live with them for awhile, but Tom flatly refuses. JUDY HAS COME TO YOU FOR SUPPORT. SHOULD THEY TAKE HIM IN? REMEMBER, THERE ARE STILL SOME YOUNGER CHILDREN AT HOME. PLEASE ADVISE.

162

# TO BARBARA
## without whom my life would be
## considerably less rewarding

# COUPLES
# in the Bible
## A Discussion Guide

Daniel R. Seagren

Contemporary Discussion Series

2448
BAKER BOOK HOUSE
Grand Rapids, Michigan